SAVING THE FISH FROM DROWNING

*For Fr Sean McFerran SDB, Founder of AFrI,
and his successors in the task of director,
Don Mullan and Joe Murray,
in recognition of all their strivings
on behalf of the little ones of this world.*

James O'Halloran SDB

Saving the Fish from Drowning

REFLECTIONS FROM THE BARRIO

with poems by Hugh O'Donnell

the columba press

First published in 2006 by
the columba press
55A Spruce Avenue, Stillorgan Industrial Park,
Blackrock, Co Dublin

Cover by Bill Bolger
Cover picture by Christine Crotty
Origination by The Columba Press
Printed in Ireland by Betaprint, Dublin

ISBN 1 85607 519 2

Copyright © 2006, James O'Halloran SDB

The Father laughs with the Son;
the Son laughs with the Father.
The Father likes the Son;
the Son likes the Father.
The Father delights in the Son;
the Son delights in the Father.
The Father loves the Son;
the Son loves the Father.
The laughter, liking, delighting,
loving is the Holy Spirit.
(Meister Eckhart)

Contents

Acknowledgements		11
Foreword *by Tom Hyland*		12
Introduction		13

PART ONE
PEACE AND JUSTICE

1.	Though the Heavens May Fall	16
	(Let Justice Be Done)	
	Go Not Gently	18
	Light	20
2.	Cause of the Century	21
	(Overcoming Poverty)	
	Beyond Tears	24
3.	And History Held Its Breath	28
	(Playing Our Part for Justice)	
	Give up your seat	30
4.	Hey Man, You a Celebrity!	31
	(Unsung Heroes of Justice)	
	The Wall	33
5.	Dear Mr President	35
	(East Timor on the brink)	
	Nothing more than Nothing	39
6.	The Light of My Eyes	41
	(Oppression in Latin America)	
	Labor Day	43
7.	Beheading the Daffodils	44
	(The Environment Issue)	
	Gardening in May	46
8.	Black Death of the 21st Century	47
	(The AIDS Pandemic)	
	Genocide	49

9.	Saving the Fish from Drowning	51
	(True Development)	
	Eucharist and Justice	54
10.	ET Phone Home	55
	(The Plight of Refugees)	
	Déjà vu	58
11.	The Earth's Our Mother	59
	(Women's Rightful Place)	
	Another View	61
	Unquietly Flows the Don	62
12.	A Search for Soulfulness	63
	(Young People Taking Their Leave)	
	Rest in Peace, Louise	66
13.	I Ask Why People Are Hungry	67
	(Religion and Politics)	
	A Hope-giving Review	70
	Hope is ...	70
14.	A Gift to the World	71
	(Africa's Sense of Community)	
	Reaching Out	74
15.	The Non-violent Alternative	75
	(Active Non-violence)	
	Christ Showing His Wounds	77
	Mayday	78
16.	Father Forgive Them	84
	(Forgiveness and Reconciliation)	
	Omagh 1998	87

PART TWO
COMMUNITY

1.	Barbarians at the Gates	90
	(Community in Disarray)	
	The Pelican	93
	The Brendan Prayer	95

2.	The Sweetness of Togetherness	97
	(The Church as Communion)	
	Spanish Point	100
	Dialogue With The Bishop	100
	I Have to Listen	102
3.	Story of a Small Christian Community	103
	Doctor and Mother	108
4.	Three Dancers One Dance	109
	(The Spirituality of Small Christian Communities)	
	My Niece Nearly Five	113
5.	Building Itself up in Love	114
	(Way Forward for the Church)	
	A Jesus Prayer	116
6.	Walking the Walk	118
	(Commitment the Soul of Community)	
	Mandla's Story	119
	The Old Man's Story	120
	The Peasant Missionaries	121
7.	Theirs Not to Reason Why	123
	(Effective Communication)	
	Trying to Boil a Kettle	125
	Sound Advice for the White Rabbit	126
8.	That They May All Be One	127
	(Unity Among Christians)	
	Eucharist and Community	130
9.	Dragging No Elephant	131
	(Ecumenism in Africa)	
	Ecumenical Pilgrimage 1996	133
10.	Building Bridges: Building Kingdom	134
	(Forging a Better World)	
	Dolores Sign of the Kingdom	137
11.	Christopher, I Owe You	138
	(Having a Sense of Process)	
	Guru of the Sixties	139

PART THREE
EDUCATION

1.	Small But Worthwhile	142
	(Education for Freedom)	
	A Small Good Thing	145
2.	Free to Soar	146
	(A Liberating Education)	
	Autumn Conference	148
3.	No Compulsion	149
	(Imaginative Educational Alternatives)	
	De-schooling	152
	Schooling	152
4.	John Bosco Educator	153
	(A Fool for Christ)	
	My Story	154
5.	The Salesian Way	156
	(Don Bosco's Preventive System)	
	A Mute Inglorious Milton	159
	Here is a man	160

Conclusion   161

Acknowledgements

I should like to express my deep gratitude to the following people who helped by reading and commenting on the manuscript: Stephen Harris, Tim Hynes, Don Mullan, Mary McDowell, Emer Ryan, Dr Michael Watts, Niamh Nolan and Yvonne O'Neill.

Foreword

Tom Hyland

I once read that the truly great and good were not to be found in the palaces and mansions of great cities. Rather are they encountered among communities in humble places. Such people are numerous in the developing world, though they can of course surface also in industrialised countries, working with people who are pushed to the margins of society.

Leaders differ. Some 'leaders' long for the power to exercise control over the lives of others, but in reality care little for their welfare. There are others, who would like to be individuals of substance, and try to do so by associating with powerful people in the hope of capturing some of their aura. Usually they are self absorbed and well-off, contenting themselves with making the odd impressive statement on behalf of the disadvantaged while doing nothing practically for them.

The problems facing us are immense. Over forty million are affected by HIV and AIDS. Meanwhile pharmaceutical companies bank huge profits while refusing to release antiretroviral drugs to victims in developing nations. Ethnic group and colour are still determining factors in deciding what refugees will be allowed to make a life in affluent societies; racist fears are stirred up by malicious people so as to frighten citizens in the host countries. As military budgets soar irrationally, poverty grows apace around the world. Civil liberties are lost with seemingly no prospect of their ever being recovered.

Despite this grim scenario, Jim O'Halloran's *Saving the Fish from Drowning* is a book of hope, which is a core value in his life. This volume is essential reading, so that we know we are not alone in our hunger for justice. We are part of a caring multitude who wish to share with the less fortunate; a multitude which realises that to ignore the oppressed in their dire need would be to determine the eventual destruction of us all.

Introduction

I have been fortunate enough to spend my working life in the stimulating areas of justice and peace, community building and education. Better still, it so happened that I was able to do this worldwide but with a predilection for Africa and Latin America. Operating in so many and such varied cultures was indeed a bonus and I can truly say that I learned far more from the people with whom I shared than I was ever able to impart.

In this volume I look back over the years and reflect on the above themes in the light of experience. This I do largely through prose pieces, which are – I hope – embellished by some fictional, non-fictional and poetic offerings. The authors of these are James O'Halloran and Hugh O'Donnell (poetry) for the most part. If another writer is quoted, they are acknowledged. Hugh O'Donnell is already a published and prize-winning poet. The sequence is as follows: an anchoring prose piece, followed by a story, apt quotation or poem that is in some way related to the piece. To be helpful, I will attach the initials H.O'D (Hugh O'Donnell) or J.O'H (James O'Halloran) to contributions where this makes for clarity.

Because the writing is influenced by experience, the work has a strong personal dimension from which it will get any uniqueness it may possess. However, I have also striven to read widely regarding the above mentioned themes. In setting down these reflections, my hope would be that it may lead people to think about these issues for themselves, whether or not they agree with me.

The Spanish word *barrio*, which occurs in the sub-title of this book, simply means 'area' or 'district'; however, it has come to be symbolic of a place that is populous, disadvantaged and yearning for justice.

Finally, I should like to point out that I am an Irish Catholic. This is my identity; this is where I come from. I would feel, however, that I am a reasonably open person who has mingled and worked with people of varying Christian denominations, members of all religions and, indeed, people who would profess no faith. I gratefully acknowledge that I learned from all of these. I would simply ask that those coming from places different from myself would consider what I say, clothe it in their own language, and see it in the light of whatever it is that gives meaning to their lives. Ultimately, all people of goodwill are on a search for the same reality – the truth that sets us free.

PART ONE

Justice and Peace

1: Though the Heavens May Fall
(Let Justice Be Done)

If relations with persons, and consequently with God, are marred by discrimination, justice is diminished, because justice consists in right relationships with self, God, neighbour and the environment. These relationships were admirably witnessed to by Jesus in his life. Without wholesome bonding there is no hope of peace. This is why the Irish bishops perceptively noted in a pastoral letter that peace is built on justice and justice is the fullness of love.[1] Often when we speak of justice, we are thinking only of social justice: fair returns for our work, proper conditions in places of employment and so on. Justice, however, is much more than that because it touches all aspects of our existence.

I once heard a woman of African origin say at a meeting in a São Paulo *favela*, or deprived district: 'I am oppressed three times over. I'm oppressed because I am poor; I'm oppressed because I am a woman; and I'm oppressed because I am black.' I was somewhat surprised to hear her say that she was oppressed because she was a woman. The men in the district were, after all, passionately involved in issues of justice. And yet this woman and others as it turned out felt downtrodden because of their gender – indeed women die in Latin America because their lives are so harsh. So apparently the menfolk lacked a clear understanding of the full nature of justice.

Respect for the environment is also an integral part of justice. There is transcendent community in God, the human community and the community of creation – all intimately bound together, all to be revered. In my experience, many women would see the oppression of nature and of themselves as intimately connected, feeling that men regard all that is specifically masculine as superior. We speak of the notion of earth as mother, but act out of that understanding when we see every flower and animal as the centre of its world with proprietary rights to its place on the planet.

1. Irish Bishops, *The Work of Justice*, Dublin: Veritas, 1977, p 9.

A poem called *Stupidity Street* by Ralph Hodgson shows how the things of nature are so precariously linked together. The poem is all the more remarkable because it was written early in the last century, when the public was certainly not as conscious of the environment issue as it is today. It says:

I saw with open eyes
Singing birds sweet
Sold in the shops,
For people to eat;
Sold in the shops of
Stupidity Street.

I saw in a vision
The worm in the wheat,
And in the shops nothing
For people to eat;
Nothing for sale
In Stupidity Street.

Cry havoc!

In her fine book, *The Cry of the People,* Penny Lernoux makes the same point, showing the havoc that reigns when multinational corporations are allowed to rape the rain forests. She writes as follows:

But perhaps the worst example of the multinationals' slash-and-burn methods in the Amazon is provided by the Italian conglomerate Liquigas, which purchased 1.4 million acres in the heart of Xavante Indians' territory. Sixty Indians died when the military forced them to move from their land, and now only a few charred stumps remain of the forests where the Xavantes once hunted, the land having been seeded in grass. Like most Amazon cattle ranches, the Liquigas project produces only for the export market, using an airstrip big enough to accommodate chartered 707s that fly direct to Italy with the meat packaged in supermarket cuts and the price stamped in lire.[2]

---

2. Penny Lernoux, *The Cry of the People*, New York, Doubleday, 1980, p 267.

And if we think about it, all this meat is leaving a country where hunger is widespread and, if Italy can be compared to other affluent nations, some of it probably ends up in trash bins. Many a time, I have seen down-and-outs gladly take out and eat whole or half-eaten sandwiches from such unsavoury places.

For environmental sensitivity, I have never forgotten lines written by the gentle William Cowper:

I would not enter on my list of friends
(Though graced with polished manners and fine sense,
Yet wanting sensibility) the man
Who needlessly sets foot upon a worm.
(The Winter Walk at Noon)

A final point about the description of justice given above is necessary. It might seem presumptuous to put right relationships with self before even relationships with God. The reasoning behind it is that, unless we can relate properly to ourselves in the first place, we are severely hindered in all other relationships. If I am not somewhat together as a person and am, for example, a bully, I can devastate the lives of others. Justice begins in our own undivided hearts.

Without justice, life becomes unliveable and peace a mirage. A well-known axiom in ethics says: 'Let justice be done, though the heavens may fall.'

* * *

Go Not Gently[3]

The girl lay in the gutter. Mike the young volunteer worker paused momentarily, conscience-stricken. His impulse was to pass by. A thousand others would have done so and easily rationalised their action.

After all, she was just another sad statistic among the millions who died yearly of starvation in the developing world and it was pointless getting worked up over one where there were so many. Better to strive so as to stop things getting this far in the first

---

3. James O'Halloran, *The Least of These* (short stories), Dublin: The Columba Press, 1991, pp 17-18.

place. Besides there was no telling what complications could arise if one intervened. It was a matter for the authorities really. The police should look into it.

But Mike was not a shirker and his thoughts were very different. Was it to pass by a case like this that he came to the developing world, equipped with a brand new diploma from the London School of Tropical Medicine? Certainly not.

He bent over the girl. She regarded him with dark sunken eyes, shining unnaturally bright with impending death. He made as though to lift her, but she shrank away from him. Either the prospect was too painful or she may have realised that she was beyond help.

She moaned and with skeletal arms slowly raised up a baby, which he had not noticed before, from the folds of her fetid garments. He took the infant from her, whereupon she smiled faintly, sighed gratefully and wearily closed her eyes.

The face of the infant moved ever so slightly. If the young mother could not be saved, maybe this tiny creature could. He would try the government hospital. Doctor Gomes would probably be on duty. He was a good man and perhaps if he injected coramine and cortisone direct to the heart, this child could be prevented from slipping away and could then be given prolonged treatment. It would be costly, but he could contact his Aunt Tilly. She had money.

He almost ran to the nearest bus-stop with his filthy little pile. People eyed him curiously, even warily, as they made way for him on the teeming street. He elbowed his way on to the crowded bus and even in those constrained circumstances people shrank away from this lad and his evil-smelling bundle.

On reaching the hospital, he rushed straight to Accident and Emergency and confronted Doctor Gomes, who was coping with a long line of patients.

'Doctor Gomes, you must help,' Mike blurted out. 'If you administer coramine and cortisone, you may save this baby and then it can be treated.'

The doctor was disconcerted for a moment by this sudden intrusion but he quickly regained his composure.

'Put the child on the table, Mike.' He examined it carefully, then paused for a second and looked compassionately at Mike's face streaming with sweat after his exertions. He quietly announced, 'This baby is dead.'

'What do you mean dead?' shouted Mike indignantly. 'If you look carefully, you'll see it's actually moving!'

Doctor Gomes gently forced the mouth of the baby open.

With bowed head Mike sank on to a chair and dug his fingers into his unruly dark curls. He sat there, defeated, and tears mingled with sweat upon his enduring blue jeans.

The tiny mouth was full of writhing worms.

Light
(for Ciaran)

My little man, down what centuries
of light did you travel
to reach us here,
your stay so short-lived.

In the twinkling of an eye
you were moving on,
bearing our name and a splinter
of the human cross we suffer.

Flashed upon us like a beacon,
we wait in darkness for that light
to come round, knowing at heart
you shine forever for us.
(H.O'D)

2: Cause of the Century
(Overcoming Poverty)

Subsisting on one dollar a day does not mean being able to afford what one dollar a day would buy when converted into local currency, but the equivalent of what one dollar would buy in the United States – a newspaper, for example, or a local bus ride. So we are told by the UNDP (2003) as they inform us that 1.17 billion hapless people on our planet 'exist' on one dollar per day. This is nearly one quarter of the world's population. And the dire news continues. Almost 800 million people, or one sixth of the people in the developing nations, suffer from malnutrition. Of these – you guessed it – 200 million are children (UN FAO 2004). And more than 100 million people in the developing countries suffer the effects of drought which leads to hunger, disease and death (World Food Programme, UN, 2003).

Statistics have a way of sanitising tragedy and of this we should be wary. The horrendous images of skeletal youngsters with bloated bellies and great accusing eyes that appear on our television screens affect us more than what are really appalling statistics; even such images, however, immunise us from the accompanying nauseating stench of disease and death. This was particularly true of the tsunami (2004) that struck Asia as I was writing these lines. But to return to those statistics: were figures to reveal proportionate numbers of indigence, hunger and death in London or New York, imagine the resulting shock and horror. Imagine the outrage!

When I started working as a priest in Latin America in the early 1970s, I was stunned one morning while reading the newspaper to learn that in desperation an Indian had been selling his blood to a blood bank to save his family from starvation. He did so continually and died as a result. There was an outcry; a commission was set up to investigate the tragedy. The bank obviously had questions to answer. A commission, however, was a wonderful mechanism that a corrupt government could use to consign an issue to oblivion! This was probably what happened. Time passed and people forgot. Never again did I see a reference to the sad event in the media. That incident affected myself more than any statistic could ever have done; for me it proved a defining moment that irrevocably opened my eyes to the reality of the situation in which I found myself.

The dire picture described above is, however, the reality on this planet. Liberal capitalism, the prevailing economic system, surely stands condemned by this situation. It is not simply that millions are marginalised from even its most minimal benefits, but many millions more are totally excluded. Cold Malthusian analysis, such as Ebenezer Scrooge applied, would regard them as surplus to requirements and, therefore, expendable. In the Latin America of the 70s, millions of people were marginalised and exploited. To be exploited one of course needs to be employed, however shabbily, but there are now countless persons who cannot even enter into the 'privileged' ranks of the exploited.

Languishing on the margins
This brings me to my main point. There is no more urgent issue for leaders in our world today than that of the deprived and dispossessed millions in our midst. If we want to foster and preserve society as such, we have to vigorously combat the selfishness that impoverishes millions throughout the world. Such selfishness leads, for example, to developing countries being bled of revenue sorely needed for health and education to service the interest on huge foreign debts – the capital sum having been paid many times over. Surely a grave injustice, being highlighted as I write by the unspeakable tsunami of 12/26 in Asia. These debts should simply be written off. An American economist with connections to the White House, whose name escapes me now, appeared on our television screens in the wake of the cataclasm to tell us, predictably, what a bad idea this would be. Then there followed the usual spin designed to turn black into white and, if possible, to deceive even the elect. The ultimate irony, of course, is that the loans made to developing countries never reached the

needy, but ended up in the Swiss bank accounts of brutal dictators and corrupt politicians. This cries out for remedying.

But credit where credit is due. As I write, the G8 has cancelled the debts of eighteen of the world's poorest countries. This is a significant beginning but lest we be carried away, there are eighty more countries in need of the same consideration. There is the fear that debt cancellation may lead certain countries to cut their aid budgets to the developing nations. And there is the realisation that the change of heart on the part of the G8 came as a result of the pressure of people power, particularly on Germany and Japan. A cogent argument for an increase in such pressure.

The late Dom Helder Camara of Brazil singled out the overcoming of poverty as the 'cause of the century'[4] (he was labelled a communist for his pains!). So not to make our contribution, however humble, to resolving this issue is to live at the margins of the history of our times. If those of us who have so much were but to reflect, we must realise that the happiness of those who have cannot be built on the misery of those who have not. Increasingly, electric fences, alarms, security gates and snarling rottweilers will be required to protect comfortable 'homes' which, after all, will then become no more than elaborate prisons or gilded cages.

On a recent visit to Johannesburg, I was deeply saddened to come across affluent areas, now largely peopled by blacks, that use barriers to keep undesirables out. And I wonder if this is the 'new apartheid' – blacks excluding blacks. Two worlds are not viable and never have been.

The question is what to do? We obviously need a commercial set-up that, instead of being market-driven, is people-centred. Natural resources are not inexhaustible, so social and human values must prevail over those that are purely economic. This would generate a genuine concern for those cut off from our economic well-being, whether they reside in the developing or developed world. We know, of course, that the problem is not

---

4. Helder Camara, *The Desert is Fertile*, London: Sheed and Ward, 1974, pp 23-41.

confined to the developing world; it is just that it is much more acute there. The gap between rich and poor in the developed world is – amazingly – greatest in the United States, one of the world's wealthiest economies. Ireland, land of the Celtic tiger, is second. I sadly cite Ireland too because it is my own country. We could perhaps look for inspiration to a place like Denmark, which is not as affluent as Ireland at the moment and has roughly a similar population, yet has, for example, a more efficient health service than we have. Their social model would undoubtedly be closer to Berlin than Boston.

Can poverty be banished from our world? Apparently so. In a syndicated article, Professor Jeffrey Sachs of Harvard University makes the exciting claim that this is possible. He writes as follows: 'If the world – especially the US and other rich countries – would shift a small amount of its military spending to meeting the need of the world's poorest peoples, our generation could free humanity from poverty's iron grip.'[5] All of us, politicians and voters, would do well to ponder and act on this.

* * *

Beyond Tears[6]
An air of foreboding hung over the tiny mud-floored home of the Jumipanta family. The father, José, and six children sat breakfasting on black coffee and dry bread, while the mother, Yolanda, huddled near an oil stove – for it was bleak – with the one-year-old Manuelito upon her knee.

The six children at table sensed something strange and, over the rims of their enamel mugs, anxiously searched the faces of their parents with great dark eyes.

Juan and Maria Taipe called on their way to work. Juan had the rope of the cargador looped over his shoulder (he would labour in the marketplace through the long day, like a beast-of-burden) and Maria had some cooked beans that she would hope-

---
5. *Sunday Times*, (South Africa), 10 March 2002, p 16.
6. James O'Halloran, *The Least of These* (short stories), Dublin: The Columba Press, 1991, pp 39-41.

fully sell, if only for a pittance.

'Today is the day?' enquired Juan.

'It is so,' replied José.

'I feel it.'

'Thank you, Juan.'

'There's no remedy.'

' 'Tis the will of God.'

'It is so.'

'Such is the life of the poor.'

Juan and Maria then patted the baby on the head and went their way. For a long time José and Maria froze in Indian stoicism.

'Will we send the children out?' asked Yolanda.

'No, little one. They must always remember how hard it was for you and me. They must share our suffering.'

The sharp-eared children looked on wonderingly.

After what seemed an eternity there was the sound of an approaching car. José looked out. A blue Mercedes was ascending the steep dirt road scattering scrawny chickens and wretched pigs noisily in its wake. Skeletal dogs moved lethargically from its wheels when death seemed imminent.

The vehicle halted outside the Jumipanta home. A pair of gringos, husband and wife, got out.

'Good day. How are you?' they greeted the family, their North American accent coming through the Spanish.

'We are well, to God be thanks,' replied José.

The gringo then conversed with his wife in English. 'There's no point in draggin' this out, honey. It's bad enough without draggin' it out.'

'I agree.'

'The baby is a sorry sight.'

'Wait till you see what a bath and shampoo will do. That dark hair will come up shining and silky. Then we'll deck him out in some nice clothes.'

The gringo went towards José, put a not unkindly hand on his shoulder and handed him a bulging envelope. 'This will help.

Don't worry. Manuelito will have a better life.'

His wife took the baby from the now trembling arms of Yolanda whose face bore an expression of infinite pain. All her tears had long drained away.

They all trooped out to the car. Eleven-year-old Pablo, the eldest child, sensed that something was gravely amiss. A tear edged down his cheek. The second eldest, Margarita, looked curiously into his face and sidled close to him. 'Adios!' shouted the gringos and waved their hands. The lady caught Manuelito's tiny arm and helped him to wave goodbye. The car departed in a cloud of dust and the little fellow looked into his mother's face with consternation as he sped away to 'a better life'.

For what seemed an age, the family remained rooted to the spot in silent tableaux. 'Let's go inside,' said José at last.

Listlessly, Yolanda poured out the remains of the morning coffee. They drank it slowly and without joy. José looked sadly at the children. 'You can go up the mountain and pick some alfalfa for the donkey.' This they loved to do, yet today they went silently, like a small funeral procession.

Outside the weather was overcast and misty. Low-lying clouds garlanded the sullen Andes; it was doubtful if the sun would show its face. José and Yolanda sat huddled wordlessly near the oil-stove.

Eventually José stood up, took some money from the envelope, threw the remainder in disgust on the floor and stalked out.

It was night when he returned – hopelessly drunk.

'Coffee,' he demanded in a truculent thick voice.

'I'll prepare some,' said Yolanda.

'Prepare!' he shouted. 'Daughter of a bitch ... should be ready ... now, now!' He set upon his wife and began to rain blows upon her. The awakened children lay petrified in their beds.

José rushed headlong out into the darkness. Yolanda turned to Pablo. 'Pablito, lock the door after me; look after the house and the children.'

'Yes mamma.'

She followed her husband as he stumbled blindly through the

night. Spent at last, he crumbled to the cheerless earth and wept bitterly.

'Little one, I had to do it. If I didn't, we'd all starve.'

'Hush, hush, I know,' she replied.

'I'm sorry, little one.' Still sobbing, he mercifully fell asleep.

Back home the children too cried themselves to sleep.

And Yolanda, her heart breaking, stayed by her man during the long dark hours.

3: And History Held Its Breath
(Playing Our Part for Justice)

If you get involved in justice and peace issues be prepared for frustration. For one thing, progress is often so slow that you have to be ready for the long haul. Often we look at the huge problems facing our world and wonder what little people like ourselves can possibly do about them, so we give up. This is exactly what we ought not to do and there are precedents to prove it.

The action of Rosa Parks would be one such precedent. This Afro-American lady refused to yield her seat on a bus to a white person in Alabama back in 1955: an unjust law demanded that she do so. After a long day's work, she told the bus-driver that she was too tired to stand. Later she was to declare that what she was really tired of was humiliation, oppression and injustice. On retreat three weeks before the historic event, taking inspiration from Jeremiah 1:7-8 where the young Jeremiah tells the Lord that he is inadequate for the role of prophet, her preacher made a telling observation. He reminded his listeners that, although they were weak, God could do great things through them. This sentiment affected her deeply, returned to her as she was asked to give up her seat and led to her refusal. She was of course arrested and thrown into prison. Yet her tiny, though valiant act of protest was the spark that ignited the mighty and successful civil rights movement of Martin Luther King Jnr.

In 1991 a bus-driver called Tom Hyland was playing cards with friends at his Dublin home in Ballyfermot. They were totally absorbed in their game but the television was flickering in the background. It so happened that the programme was dealing with a notorious massacre of innocent civilians by Indonesian soldiers in an East Timorese graveyard. Just as Hitler illegally invaded and occupied Poland in 1939, so did Indonesia invade the newly independent East Timor in 1975. Two years previously, East Timor had won its independence from Portugal.

While waiting for a companion who was pondering what

card to play, Tom glanced momentarily at the programme. It grabbed his attention. He continued watching. His companions joined him. Tom was appalled by what he saw and went on to found a group or better a movement, entitled East Timor Solidarity Ireland. As East Timor strove successfully to cast off the yoke of the invader, there was no more effective advocate for their cause than East Timor Solidarity Ireland. Tom was an unlikely hero. He says of himself that he used to drive past the US Embassy in Ballsbridge on his bus route and see people protesting outside over various issues. He thought they were 'wacko'. But then he saw priests and nuns among them and it set him thinking; if priests and nuns were protesting about something, there must be a good reason for it. When he saw that defining programme, he didn't say, 'Somebody should do something about this', but rather, 'I should do something about this!' The little he could do he did by starting the solidarity group. You could say that he paused in his card game and history held its breath.

Even the slightest gesture
I think the stories of Rosa Parks and Tom Hyland can greatly encourage us. Instead of feeling overwhelmed by situations of injustice, we should do even the little we can to counteract them. There is no telling where our small gestures will end, so let us not just go back to the game of cards.

As we said above, justice is a matter of right relationships with myself, God, fellow human beings and all creation. It begins in my own heart, home and community. If it doesn't begin in those places, we are never likely to go to the barricades in the cause of right. However, whatever we do, no matter how insignificant, to foster right relationships in the world will be well done. A small lamp will have been lit whose light will shine through the darkness over vast distances, for even an ocean of darkness cannot extinguish a small glimmer of light.

* * *

Give up your Seat

Some you can never put down
with a rifle butt to the head
or a bayonet urged against the seam,
by hanging, flogging, abandonment at three.

You put them down, they come up for air,
add more rocks to the bulging postbag
but the bubbles continue to rise,
you slap your face in despair.

Consult then, arrange a fee,
the inquisitor high on coke
(scalpel, scorpion, ECT)
squinting at the keyhole of the soul.

For they will look you in the eye
though you flick the eyeball out,
will smile in a smashed mouth,
reach out when you have blown off the shoulder

at close range, walk into your study
with chains on their ankles and wrists
creaking like rusted machines –
give up your seat to them.
(H.O'D)

4: Hey Man, You a Celebrity!
(Unsung Heroes of Justice)

I had a moving experience in Washington DC. It was related to an Afro-American lady called Betty. Betty who? I never got her surname: she was a waitress in Burger King. While staying with friends in Washington during the summer of 1999, I was offered the possibility of attending a reception for Rosa Parks, who was being awarded the Congressional Medal of Honour. As a speaker later remarked facetiously at the function for her, she had already been honoured by God, the saints and angels, the great American public and now – at long last – she was being recognised by the US Congress! I went to the reception in the company of a girl from Northern Ireland who, I have it on good authority, was the first to interest Bill Clinton in the Northern Ireland issue while he was still Governor of Arkansas. I had just launched a first novel entitled *When the Acacia Bird Sings* in Washington and this girl insisted on my bringing a copy to give to Rosa Parks. I was understandably reluctant to do this, but the persuasiveness of Rita M – the girl's name – was too much for me. I could see how Bill Clinton was won over to the cause of peace in Northern Ireland! The poor man didn't stand a chance.

We had to wait for quite a time for Rosa to arrive. While doing so, I chatted at length with an Afro-American man who was obviously part of Rosa's security detail. There was a buzz of anticipation when Rosa entered. She was elderly, frail and in a wheelchair. Her speech was delivered on her behalf by another lady. They were, however, still the words of Rosa and what an inspirational figure she was.

When the function was finished, Rosa was surrounded by burly bodyguards, both male and female. There was no way through the circle. I told the security man to whom I had been chatting how I had a book for Rosa; also I carried greetings from an Irish friend of hers.

'Take a look, man,' he said, 'can't be reached no how. Stay

where you are or you will be trampled on.' He disappeared into the mass. After interminable minutes, the crowd parted like the Red Sea. At one end of the parting sat Rosa Parks, at the other stood myself. My security friend beckoned me forward. I presented the book to her and greeted her on behalf of the Irish friend. Then I left the place in a daze and went to Burger King for a cup of coffee. Betty was there.

At first I was in such a euphoric state that I didn't notice her. I felt I had met, not only one of the great women of the twentieth century, but a very spiritual person. In her presence you were possessed by a profound feeling of peace. Gradually, however, Betty's up-beat voice began to impinge on my consciousness. She was circulating among the customers, spreading goodwill wherever she went with a cheery word for everyone. At one table she surprised a girl by approaching with a birthday cake topped with blazing candles. She then got everyone singing *Happy Birthday* and made a hearty fuss of the blissful young woman. And so it went.

Eventually she stood at my own table. 'Hi! And how are you today, sir?' she asked perkily.

'Very well, thank you, Betty.' The name was on her lapel.

'You visiting Washington?' She had detected the Irish accent.

'Yes, here visiting friends.'

'Enjoyin' yourself?'

'Immensely. It's a wonderful place.' Then, unable to contain myself, I added, 'You'll never guess who I've just met.'

'Tell me!'

'Rosa Parks.'

'ROSA PARKS!'

'None other.'

'Hey man, you a celebrity!' I winced a little.

'Betty, to me every human being is a celebrity. You're certainly one. I've seen the happiness you've been spreading in this restaurant. I'm sure you've made their day for many people coming in here. You may even have made somebody's life.'

You will not be surprised to hear that Betty looked amazed.

The small gestures of Rosa Parks and Tom Hyland had considerable historical impact and their results are well known. Not so those of Betty. I believe, however, that her efforts are just as significant and that there is no telling their outcome. It is people like her, doing their little routine best, that keep this world turning on its axis. And mostly they are women.

* * *

The Wall[7]

Forty million people would die of hunger that year. So the teacher said. And while forty million were dying of hunger more than one million dollars would be spent every minute on armaments that could annihilate the human race. If the manufacture of those horrendous weapons were halted for only two weeks each year, the basic food and medical problems of the world could be solved for the entire year.

The dark young eyes of his audience flashed with indignation. What the teacher was saying was for them only too real, because the spectral people around them were daily stalked by hunger and early death. Indeed they themselves knew the pangs of want, but they felt hopeless in the face of this overwhelming problem.

The teacher went to the blackboard and slowly started to draw. When he finished, there was the picture of a massive forbidding wall.

'Tell me,' he said to the young people, 'do you sacrifice yourself in any way for your deprived brothers and sisters?'

'Well,' began Marcelo tentatively, 'I teach in a night-school for illiterates.' The teacher put a tiny crack in the obscene wall.

'I help in a medical dispensary at weekends,' said René. Another tiny crack.

'And I try to counsel small kids who sniff glue,' chimed in Adriana. Still a further crack.

Narcisa ran a club for children, Mario a magazine for his area,

---

7. James O'Halloran, *The Least of These*, Dublin: The Columba Press, 1991, p 26.

Pedro organised summer camps and Magdalena worked in a shop and tried to treat the customers cheerfully and with respect. The Teacher went on drawing.

'Suppose,' he said, 'enough plain people all over the world through their acts of significant sharing, however humble, go on making cracks in this great monolith of selfishness, what will become of the wall?'

Hope dawned in their eyes.

5: Dear Mr President
(East Timor on the Brink)

The people of East Timor were threatened with genocide at the hands of militias opposed to their independence from Indonesia. So the media reported. It was Saturday, 11 September 1999. I stood appalled in my office. 'This can't be!' I thought. 'Somebody has to do something.' There followed a disturbing question: Why not *me*? Predictably there were the rationalisations. What could an ordinary person like myself do in the face of such calamities? It was up to the big international players to act. They should really do something to stop this unfolding tragedy. But conscience went on troubling me. There must be something you can do yourself, it urged, however small.

Then I thought of the All Ireland Senior Hurling Final that was being played the following afternoon between Kilkenny and Cork. I was an ardent Kilkenny fan and had a marvellous ticket for the Hogan Stand and had rushed back from abroad to be present. If I got involved in this East Timorese issue, I might well end up having to give the All Ireland a miss. Every Kilkenny person lives each year in the hope that their team will be in the All Ireland, and win it. It's a raw tribal urge. Imagine the torment I went through. My nobler part conquered, however, because, when it became an issue of attending the All Ireland or saving lives, there could, realistically, be no contest. If I were to miss the final, so be it.

Yet the question as to what to do still remained. It was then I thought of Ann Edwards. Ann was President Clinton's Advance Press Secretary and I had met her on a visit to Washington in the summer of 1996. I was spending some time with friends Adrian O'Neill, his wife Aisling and children Tomás and Aoife. Adrian was a diplomat at the Irish Embassy in Washington and, through Ann, organised a White House visit for me. Ann herself kindly showed us round and treated us to soft drinks in her office afterwards. I then had a conversation with her, which gave me a chance to get to know her better, and I found her a most friendly person.

And so it was on that fateful night of Saturday, 11 September 1999, the thought suddenly came to me: Why not phone Ann Edwards? I had read in the media that East Timor Solidarity Ireland Campaign had been urging the United States and others to intervene on behalf of the East Timorese. Before trying to ring Ann I felt I should call Tom Hyland, the founder of that organisation (cf chapter 3). Luckily, Tom was available. It wasn't always easy to track down such a busy man. I found him quite downhearted. The latest news from East Timor was bad. The militias were killing people. Some of them had even managed to enter the United Nations Compound in Dili and shot people being harboured there. Tom had received a call that day from an East Timorese friend of ours, José Belo, a relative of Archbishop Belo; José was in the United Nations Compound and rang – to say goodbye. He didn't expect to come out alive from that place. Tom urged him not to lose hope; we would do our best to get him out. He replied that even if he wanted to he couldn't leave because his wife and child were there with him. I then told Tom about my idea of phoning Ann Edwards. He eagerly encouraged me to do so and mentioned that East Timor Solidarity Ireland had sent an emissary to Washington, urging the Americans to intervene and save the East Timorese. The emissary, however, only managed to see some minor functionary in the State Department.

I phoned Ann. The phone rang and rang. If Tom Hyland was hard to contact, imagine how slim were the chances of reaching the even busier Advance Secretary of the President of the United States. I was about to give up when a man said 'Hello!' It was her husband Tom, whom I was relieved to hear say, 'Just a minute and I'll get her for you.'

When Ann came on, we engaged in the customary pleasantries and small talk for a while. Then I said, 'Ann, there's something I really need to speak to you about.'

'Oh I guessed you weren't just calling by the way.'

'It's about East Timor.'

'I know, I know, but if East Timor breaks away from Indonesia that whole archipelago could start falling apart.'

'But, Ann, East Timor was never a part of Indonesia; it was a Portuguese colony that declared independence from Portugal in 1975. It was invaded by Indonesia that same year as illegally as was Poland by Germany in 1939. Indeed on 7 December 1975, the United Nations Security Council called on Indonesia to withdraw its troops from East Timor.'

Anne considered this and, knowing I was a Catholic priest, asked me how the church was faring.

'Archbishop Belo has been exiled and Bishop do Nascimento beaten up. We feel that there is a window of opportunity of about a week for a force to go in and prevent genocide.'

At this point I sensed that I was getting through to Ann and I went on to tell her about my friend José Belo and what was happening in East Timor as we spoke.

'Look,' she said, 'there are people in the administration who think as you do on this problem. There is in fact a general who shares your sentiments. I'll tell you what. Write a letter saying those things that you have said, fax it to me and I'll have it on the President's desk in the morning.'

I was dumbfounded. And I started backpedalling. 'Ann, there is a man here in Dublin called Tom Hyland, the founder of East Timor Solidarity Ireland Campaign, he is really the one who should write this letter on behalf of the organisation.'

'I know that you in Ireland are more informed than most on this East Timor issue. Let both of you write letters and I will have them on the President's desk in the morning,' she repeated. This good woman was certainly playing her part.

Once Ann had rung off, I got back to Tom Hyland. Since he was the better informed, we agreed that he would compose the letter and we would both sign it. It was written on the official notepaper of East Timor Ireland Solidarity Campaign, which figured a long list of distinguished patrons, and was dated 12 September 1999. The reason was that it was being hastily written after midnight; it was now Sunday. It read as follows:

East Timor Ireland Solidarity Campaign
24-26 Dame Street
Dublin 2

President William J. Clinton
The White House
Washington

12th September 1999

Dear President Clinton,
We write to you as campaigners for human rights from the elation of the independence vote [in the East Timorese referendum] to the despair of recent events.

On Wednesday night, we received a telephone call from inside the UNAMET compound in Dili, the capital of East Timor. It came from a very dear Timorese friend, José Belo. José came to Ireland earlier this year to study peace and reconciliation. He met many people involved in Northern Ireland's peace process in which you have had such a crucial role.

José rang to say goodbye. We told him that we would do everything we could to get him out, but he informed us that, even if we could get him out, he could not leave his wife and child behind. We have had no further correspondence from José and do not know if he and his family have survived.

Mr President, as individuals who have been deeply impressed with your involvement in the Irish peace process we are pleading with you to help stop the killing of a most wonderful and gentle people, the East Timorese.

We remember your inauguration on the television and were delighted that you had been elected President of the United States of America. What will be forever etched on our memories is Michael Bolton's song, 'It's Been A Long Time Coming'. We were close to tears watching and listening, but the knowledge that you had been elected President lifted the spirits of all campaigners for human rights.

Mr President, we ask and plead with you to intervene and save the lives of the East Timorese people. They have suffered so much.

Thank you for reading our letter.
Yours sincerely,

Tom Hyland   (Fr) Jim O'Halloran
Co-ordinator   *Spiritual Director*

On 20 September 1999 the Australian-led peacekeeping troops of the International Force for East Timor (INTERFET), with crucial logistical backing from the Americans, went into East Timor on behalf of the United Nations to stop the killings and smooth the road to the country's declaration of independence. Tom Hyland believes the above letter played a decisive role in that outcome.

The foregoing makes the point once more that no effort is too small in the cause of justice. From minute mustard seeds great trees grow. By the way, I made the All Ireland Final, but Cork beat my team Kilkenny. Still it's only a game (aaarrrgh!). As some cynic said, 'No good deed goes unpunished.' Thankfully, José Belo and his family survived.

* * *

Nothing more than Nothing
Once upon a time there were two birds sitting on a branch of a tree. One was a dove and one was a titmouse (a small gray bird, sort of like a sparrow). They were sitting and talking about all the things that were going on in the world. They had heard stories from all over as they migrated and visited with other birds, and they were exchanging the news. Then, as was their habit, they began to discuss philosophy and theology and politics. But after a while they became bored with that.

Then it began to snow. It was the kind of snow that brought fat, fluffy flakes. The dove looked at the titmouse and asked: 'Do you know how much a snowflake weighs?'

The titmouse thought about it for a while and said, 'No, I

never thought about it.'

'Well,' said the dove, 'I think it weighs nothing more than nothing. I mean, look at the snow floating down, these fat, soft, fluffy flakes.'

The titmouse thought about it some more and said, 'If you think a snowflake weighs nothing more than nothing, I have a little story to tell you. Once when I was sitting on a branch, just like this one, I didn't have anything to do. It started to snow, so I began counting snowflakes, fat and fluffy ones just like these. I counted a lot, a couple of hundred, a couple of thousand. I got up to one million, eight hundred and forty-six thousand, six hundred and twenty-two snowflakes and then, one snowflake – which you say weighs nothing more than nothing – floated down, landed on my branch, and cracked it straight through. The branch went falling to the ground, and I had to fly off.'

With that, the titmouse flew off and left the dove sitting alone on the branch.

(Megan McKenna)

6: The Light of My Eyes
(Oppression in Latin America)

'Four hundred years of colonialism; one-hundred-and-sixty of the same!' It rhymes better in Spanish: *Cuatrocientos años de colonialismo; cientosesenta años de lo mismo!* So said the placard of a small protesting group amid all the animated celebrations in a Latin American country that was marking the one-hundred-and-sixtieth annniversary of gaining independence from Spain.

Before ever becoming a priest, I spent some years in Latin America in the nineteen fifties. Later I was to return for many more years after ordination. I grew to love Latin America and its people; what I am going to say here, therefore, I say in the fond hope that it may prove helpful.

Marginalised and excluded
The above-mentioned slogan contained a truth that sadly persists to this day. Independence from Spain brought wealth and power to a small, largely white-skinned minority, while the overwhelming mostly dark-skinned majority have been kept in thrall. The growth of militarism, due in no small way to the exploits of men like Simon Bolivar, also complicated the situation, as army elites for the most part aligned themselves with the oligarchy in maintaining the *status quo*. They were not shy either of interfering in matters of state and indeed in seizing power when they deemed it necessary – Chile under Pinochet would be a case in point. As far as I could see, armies created states within states and were more about suppressing their own peoples than fighting foreign wars. There was even suspicion of collusion between military elites in different countries when one or other was in political difficulties at home. The neighbour would conveniently mass troops on the border, leading to the declaration of a national emergency to take the minds of people off local problems – cunning devils!

Brutal military dictatorships held sway from 1960-1985. Then formal democracy was introduced insofar as people voted every four years, but it was only formal. For democracy to work you need true democrats and they were in short supply; rather did you have autocratic civilian bosses who failed to deliver a better life for the mass of the people, showing more zeal in augmenting their bank accounts. Understandably the people grew disillusioned and the number of those voting decreased. So one form of *caciquismo* (having bosses) was replaced by another. Unless politicians become convinced democrats, democracy will never take root in Latin America. Civic and church bodies have to make a great effort to promote young politicians who are honest people and true patriots. We of course know that this is no easy matter and we will never do it perfectly; even in old western democracies corruption has arisen. It is when the rule of law does not prevail that we are in real trouble.

During my time in Latin America, the situation was bad for the marginalised masses, who were shamefully exploited. The tragedy is that today matters are much worse. With the growth of the free-market economy Latin Americans are lucky if they are exploited, because millions of people are now, not just exploited, which means that they have employment of some kind, but totally excluded. To put it bluntly, they are irrelevant.

The free market – dominant market would be more accurate – is pushed largely by the affluent world. This developed world has always been a factor in Latin America's malaise, because the ruling elite within the sub-continent have been in cahoots with those outside forces in frustrating the democratic rights of plain people. The sad fact is that the countries of the developed world have shown more interest in promoting trade with Latin America than in furthering democracy. To their shame they have even cosied up to brutal dictatorships in so doing.

Let me personalise the distress of ordinary people by relating something I read while I was in that part of the world. A taxi driver put the corneas of his eyes up for sale in an effort at finding money to feed and educate his children. Friends remonstrated with him, 'But Pedro, you will lose the light of your eyes!' To which he replied, 'My wife and children are the light of my eyes.' What to do in the face of such desperation?

Remedies

Firstly, the poor will have to be empowered politicially and the elite come to accept this. That way lies the well-being of all Latin Americans. If the downtrodden are not included in the power structure, they may force their way in violently. That the poor will win power, however, is surely a historic inevitability; we saw it happen in South Africa. A lid cannot be kept on boiling rage forever.

The ending of poverty would also be mandatory. This is by no means the utopia that many would have us believe. In this regard, we might recall the words of Professor Jeffrey Sachs of Harvard already quoted: 'If the world – especially the US and other rich countries – would shift a small amount of its military spending to meeting the needs of the world's poorest people, our generation could free humanity from poverty's iron grip.' And needless to say, the reduction of the hefty military budgets within Latin America itself would bring considerable relief to the subcontinent.

The peace and happiness that would result from including the oppressed in the democratic process and ending poverty could not be achieved by all the armaments of the world.

* * *

Labor Day

> A Vietnamese mother and her son
> approached our picnic on shy feet
> asking to search the bin
> for our empty bottles and cans.
>
> In exchange she left us
> a memory of twelve baskets full
> of scraps gathered on tiptoe.
> (H.O'D)

7: Beheading the Daffodils
(The Environmental Issue)

Just last evening I saw two swallows fly the length of an adjacent park instinctively on their way to nest in some precise Irish destination – barn, shed or storied castle. Quite possibly they were near ending a wearying journey from the southern-most tip of Africa. I often saw them gather on telegraph wires there, all a-twitter, as they gathered strength and courage for the momentous ordeal. My heart always leaps as the swallows arrive. I am fortunate to live near the park in what is a populous area of Dublin. It gives me a lot of joy as I see the seasons come and go: the young green of spring, the vivid yellows, reds and russets of autumn.

As well as giving me joy, the park is also a source of sorrow, not because it offends in any way, but on account of what happens to it. No sooner do the daffodils toss their golden heads in the breezes of spring than they are often beheaded by wanton children. Or worse still, you may see a tree that has been several years a-growing condemned to a slow death, because its bark has been cruelly ringed by a knife. The park workers usually remove the tree immediately and plant another in its place as they relentlessly, and indeed successfully, combat vandalism. Yet one mourns the wasted years. And who is to say that the flowers and trees aren't somehow aware of their fate? Are people who talk to flowers that eccentric? All of us come from dust and in his *Short History of Nearly Everything*, Bill Bryson reminds us humans that, if all our minutest components were picked apart with a tweezers (ouch!), only a pile of dust would remain.

Of a piece
The human community, the community of creation and, from a religious perspective, the community of the Trinity are all intimately linked. What happens to one impacts the three. The environmental issue is now vying in importance with poverty for the

attention of justice devotees. How tragic, then, that we abuse the environment, often ignorant of the havoc we are causing. It's not just that children behead the daffodils; worse still adults through their business practices and political decisions are 'beheading the world'. Sadly greed takes precedence over environmental common sense. This is of course suicidal and, through our rape of the planet, we will make it uninhabitable for our children and grandchildren, if we do not take urgent action to remedy the situation. It is already only minutes from midnight.

I wonder why religious leaders aren't more voluble about this. Actions that poison the air and pollute the waterways are not merely careless or wayward, they are sinful. They harm present generations and disinherit future ones. This is sinful and we need to say so.

Many of the offending nations are Christian in name yet lack the appreciation for creation that Jesus showed when he uttered words of unsurpassing beauty like:

Consider the lilies of the field, how they grow;
they toil not, neither do they spin:
And yet I say unto you,
that even Solomon in all his glory
was not arrayed like one of these.
(Matthew 6:28)

Other religions show a similar regard for the planet. I found, for instance, a profound reverence for creation among Buddhists. In Thailand I learned of eight members from a Buddhist community cycling through the country in order to persuade people of the dire need to preserve the rain forests. That community was also farming in an environmentally friendly fashion on the banks of the river Kwai, just below the site of the famous bridge – which wasn't quite a bridge in reality. Interestingly, though the river had fish, the community was vegetarian. They also had a flock of geese on the river which were not used for food. They were cherished because of the community's love of creation. In fact, as I lay awake on the deck of a boathouse, watching the moon forge a golden path across the river, two ganders that did not share the peaceful ways of the community battled over a likely goose and had to be quarantined in the interests of law and order!

So what to do if we want to solve the environmental crisis? Regarding the children, we should instil in them a love of nature at home and in school. I know this is already being done but we have to redouble our efforts. Then adults and children alike must rate people, trees, daffodils and koala bears far above money and power. We will regard them as partners in this world, for this is what they are, and not as objects for our unbridled use. It is as simple and complex as that.

* * *

Gardening in May

The heart-breaking stuff over,
there is now a compatible air
to encourage green. Just now
a man driving a lawn mower
has disappeared behind some trees
assuring us that everything
is under control. It's a show

of force, all this industry,
a clear statement that we are
alive and notice grass coming on
strong, leaves stirring ...
but mainly it's the old year
we inhabit where lives linger
neither happy nor supremely sad.

For seasons are like children,
craving our attention,
showing off their poems
and early steps. We indulge
their promise for a time
until the pressure builds
and we rush out to murder daisies.
(H.O'D)

8: Black Death of the 21st Century
(The AIDS Pandemic)

Here and there a bicycle or a motor cycle lay rusting because the generation that used them were all dying or dead. I speak of a village in Tanzania that was decimated by AIDS; only the old and very young were in evidence. When in South Africa in 2003, I was told that in the foreseeable future the country would have one million orphans owing to the pandemic. At the moment many orphaned children are being taken care of by their grandparents but soon there will no longer be grandparents to fall back on. A friend, who now runs a wonderful centre for youth formation, anticipates that the centre will, instead, soon be filled with orphans. In Zimbabwe I found people simply numbed by all the funerals; the cemetery at the little town of Marondera always had twenty newly dug graves at the ready. I entered an adobe hut on the outskirts of Addis Ababa where a woman lay dying, obviously from the dread disease. Two families occupied the one-room adobe hut and I was so upset that I put my hand in my pocket and gave the wasting mother – the father had deserted the family – what I had. Futile gesture in many ways!

No doubt about it, AIDS has now taken its place alongside poverty and the environment as a crucial global issue. The effects of AIDS are being felt most acutely in Africa, where they are exacerbated by deprivation, hunger and cultural practices. Africa also cannot afford the antiretroviral drugs to counter the pandemic as wealthy nations can. The manufacturers of these drugs have been reluctant to lower their prices in the face of the catastrophe, though there are signs that this may be changing. And the malady is not confined to Africa; it is a worldwide reality.

Remedies?
What to do in the face of this scourge? There is much debate around the issue. In South Africa emphasis has been given to the use of condoms; the slogan has been, 'Be wise, condomise!'

Influential figures have recommended them and there have been campaigns in the media promoting their use. There is no doubt that condoms do give protection, but not complete protection. They are fallible and not even the manufacturers, when pressed, will make that claim – I actually saw a letter from one multinational corporation that admitted as much. The failure rate is given variously as 10% or as high as 30% – not of course by any multinational corporation. Either way there is a considerable risk. So to encourage sole and unconsidered use of this means of AIDS prevention would not seem to be a prudent procedure. Indeed dropping condoms on schools from helicopters – as has happened – only encourages promiscuity, which is the greatest cause of AIDS. It is noteworthy that, despite the ready availability of condoms in South Africa, 25% of the population are HIV positive. This disappointing statistic has not been dented.

There are places where statistics have commenced to drop, such as Kenya, Uganda and Zambia. In these parts a programme entitled 'Education for Life', which gets government support, has put the emphasis on abstinence, self control and fidelity to one partner, in addition to a prudent use of condoms in specific situations. It encourages young people to discipline themselves. In my experience this would in fact be the typical viewpoint of the ordinary thinking African. The dreaded affliction is largely driven by men. Women are expected to be true to their husbands, while society has been tolerant of male infidelity. A cultural transformation is called for here and cultural changes are stubborn. But the choice is stark: life or death. I believe that Africa and the rest of the world will choose life over death and this could lead to a regeneration of Africa and, indeed, of the world.

Regarding the dire situation of women with respect to AIDS in Africa, the following are telling comments taken from a meeting on the subject of the disease in 2003:

'My husband dropped me here. Now he has gone off. I'll not see him until midnight. What is he doing in the meantime? It is not the women who are the problem; it is the men.' ... 'There should be a workshop for the men.' ... 'A woman said to me that capital punishment is done away with in South Africa. But not for women. We live with the death penalty.'

The case of a family in Kenya always stays in my mind. A young mother with two children was working at a mission station where I was staying. Not seeing a father, I asked the priest in charge of the place if he were dead. He told me he was. Then I began to wonder as to the cause of his death and asked the same person if it was AIDS. He quietly confirmed this. It was in fact the reason why he had given the young mother employment. I further enquired whether the mother was also infected to which he replied, 'Yes – and both the children.' Within five years, all three were dead. The father had passed on the infection to the whole family.

There are those who say that control is fine but unrealistic. This of course takes a very dim view of the capabilities of human beings and thousands of Africans are proving it false, as, indeed, are countless others throughout the planet. There is one important difference between the AIDS pandemic of the 21st century and the Black Death of the Middle Ages. The people in those times did not know that it was rats with fleas aboard that were causing the plague, so it wreaked unbridled havoc. Today we are much more enlighted and the means of putting an end to the catastrophe are within our control.

* * *

Genocide

The black sky was pregnant with snow. But it was too bitter for snow. Around the yard under watchful eyes swirled hundreds of people, exercising to keep warm. Upon their breasts they bore the stigmatising Star of David. On three sides the space was surrounded by grim walls and on the fourth by tall bars.

A young, dark-eyed woman moved mechanically with the rest, her face contorted in silent agony. By her side was a six-year-old. He had the woman's large mystical eyes and looked out upon the world, fearful, uncomprehending. The woman momentarily raised her own tortured eyes to Yahweh. She then quickly removed the Star of David from the little boy, and slipped him through the imprisoning bars. 'Run, son,' she begged.

'Where will I run to, mamma?' pleaded the six-year-old.

'I don't know, Ben,' she cried with a broken heart. 'But please, oh please, run! RUN!'

And he ran he knew not where in Prague's gathering gloom. Most of the swirling mass moved forward unheeding of the poignant drama as they walked the treadmill that led to – Auschwitz.

9: Saving the Fish from Drowning
(True Development)

Development, closely related to justice, is a notion that is often misunderstood. Even well meaning people fall into serious blunders in this regard. A traditional story that I first came upon in Tanzania will illustrate this.

Long, long ago in our land there was a rainy season such as had never been seen before, or since, for that matter. The water was everywhere and the animals were running up the hills to escape it. So fast did the floods come that many of them drowned, except for the monkeys, who smartly climbed to the tree-tops to avoid the rising water. From their vantage point they looked down on the raging waters and to their consternation saw the fish swimming and jumping about in the flood. The creatures seemed to be enjoying themselves yet it had to be a false impression, the monkeys concluded. In reality those unfortunate souls were in a dangerous situation.

One of the monkeys called out to a companion, 'Look down, my friend, at these poor creatures. They are going to drown. Do you see how they are fighting for their lives?'

'Yes, indeed,' replied the other monkey.

'What a shame! It was impossible for them to escape to the hills because they don't seem to have any legs. But what can we do to save them?'

'Let me see. If we wade in at the edge of the flood, where the waters aren't deep enough to cover us, maybe we can help them to get out.'

So all the monkeys did just that. With much difficulty they caught the fish one by one and placed them on dry land. After a time, there was a great pile of them lying on the grass – all of them motionless.

'Do you see how tired these creatures are?' asked one of the monkeys. 'They are just sleeping and resting now. Had it not been for us, my friends, all these poor people without legs would have drowned.'

'Yes,' observed another, 'they were trying to escape us because they couldn't understand our good intentions but, when they wake up, they will be very grateful because we have brought them salvation.'

Misguided efforts
Like the monkeys in this story, our efforts at development, though well meaning, are often totally misguided. By taking people's destiny out of their own hands we do the equivalent of saving the fish from drowning. In other words we help in ways that do more harm than good. In Africa I have seen heavy machinery rotting in ditches for want of fuel or a spare part. I have seen a once proud hospital with trees growing out through the windows of what was formerly the operating theatre. These were projects that expatriates thought would be beneficial for the area yet failed to dialogue with the local people about them. They were never really the projects of the local inhabitants. They never owned them. A shame this because in the end people cannot be developed; they must develop themselves. The question is whether there isn't something outsiders can do to assist this process. If so, well and good. The trouble is that too often we expatriates go in with the answers and not the questions; we talk but we do not listen. It is so important to listen carefully to what people are saying, whether it be in society or the churches. It is there that true development starts because people have to be in charge of their own progress. It is hard for even well disposed development personnel to shake off the conviction that they know best.

In the mid-nineties I met a person in Ethiopia who had recently worked in a department of the United States government. He told me that there were two objectives where Africa was concerned: the promotion of free trade and multi-party democracy. Free trade, I felt, the developing world needed like the Dead Sea needs salt. It is fine for strong economies yet lethal for the weak. A simple girl in Bolivia taught me this in one easy lesson. She explained how imports from the United States undercut the modest prices charged for locally manufactured clothing, thereby putting Bolivians out of work. As for instant multi-party democracy, how instant was the growth of democracy in the developed world? Desirable though it may be, there is a process in its development that must be respected and, ultimately, people have to do it for themselves. As I write, President Bush and Prime Minister Blair are proposing democracy for the world. I wonder what precisely they have in mind?

Our common understanding of democracy is that you have a government party or parties in power and a party or parties in opposition. Is this the only expression of democracy? In traditional African society there was an assembly, presided over by a chief. In this assembly decisions were arrived at through dialogue and consensus and articulated by the chief who listened carefully to the debate. Opposing viewpoints were processed respectfully in this system and there were constructive means for removing an unsatisfactory chief. Within the ethnic group there was a figure known as the Public Vituperator. Custom allowed him to offer whatever criticisms he thought fit to the chief and he was obliged to listen. The Public Vituperator was somewhat like our Ombudsman. The question arises then as to whether there isn't a communal approach to democracy. After all, in our system 51% of the vote beats 49%, which can leave a lot of people unsatisfied.

Local competence

Workers in the developing nations are not lacking in ingenuity. They cannot afford to be; they have to survive. While walking through a township of Nairobi some years ago, I saw cooking stoves which were manufactured locally and perfectly adapted to the needs of the residents.

And in Zimbabwe I was shown a whole array of unsophisticated farm implements and machinery that were most suited to the environment. Indeed the genius of Africans is plain to see in their arts and crafts.

From the foregoing, it is obvious that we have to approach the issue of development with much more circumspection, humility and by listening to people with the utmost care. These qualities, together with economic fair play, will prevent us from engaging in the futile exercise of saving the fish from drowning.

* * *

Eucharist and Justice
The eucharist demands a world where there is universal collaboration and equality among people. It is, therefore, intimately linked not just to purely spiritual issues, but also to political, social and economic ones. The justice element here is obvious. Christ generously breaks bread with the whole world and we are challenged to do the same, especially with refugees and the 40 million who die of hunger or hunger-related diseases every year; a number that corresponds to the combined populations of Belgium, Canada, and Australia. And this tragedy is befalling people in a world of plenty. As often happens, most of the victims are children.[8]

---

8. James O'Halloran SDB, *Small Christian Communities, Vision and Practicalities*, Dublin: The Columba Press, 2002, p 50.

10: ET Phone Home
(The Plight of Refugees)[9]

Refugees, asylum-seekers and migrants are to our days what pilgrims and wandering minstrels were to the Middle Ages. Only they are vastly more numerous and whereas the wanderers of medieval times were considered exotic – even bohemian – those of the modern era are often looked upon with fear and suspicion. These sentiments, as we will see, are largely unfounded.

To qualify for refugee status a person must have a 'well-founded fear of being persecuted for reasons of race, religion, nationality, membership of a particular social group or political opinion.' They must be outside of the country of their nationality and unable to avail of the protection of that country. They could also be prevented from seeking protection of the country of their nationality because of the well-founded fear mentioned above (cf UN 1951 Refugee Convention). An asylum seeker is a person who has applied for refugee status and whose claim is being examined. Migrants are people outside of their own country for whatever reason.

In the case of the refugee, the implication of the UN understanding of the term is that they must have crossed an international frontier. This can cause great hardship because millions of refugees in the world are internal ones; they are in fact refugees within their own countries and, consequently, not regarded legally as refugees by the United Nations. This deprives them of a variety of entitlements. In Ethiopia following the civil war that ended in 1991, I came across thousands of internal refugees living in shanty conditions on the verge of Addis Ababa. Mostly they were mothers and children, the fathers having fled the harsh conditions and established second families elsewhere. From the United Nations' point of view they were not officially refugees and therefore did not qualify for aid, though

---

9. cf James O'Halloran, *When the Acacia Bird Sings*, Dublin: The Columba Press, 1999. Poignant refugee story.

their lot was more bitter than that of many *bona fide* refugees. Their own government was urging them to go back to their homes in Tigray or wherever but there were no homes to go to. They had been laid waste in the war. To me they seemed deserving of a helping hand because they were active in their cause. Those valiant women strove to find jobs, however humble, so as to keep their families together. They also endeavoured to maintain their hovels clean and tidy. Some had even set up stalls, selling a few sorry-looking tomatoes and vegetables. I really feel that the United Nations should also be concerned about the plight of internal refugees, despite their lack of official refugee status.

The tragedy unfolding in Sudan's Darfur, as I write, would be a further example of this crisis. Many are being killed even with the collusion of their own government who ought to be protecting them. Others are dying of disease and hunger while relief is excruciatingly slow in coming. The foot-dragging of the United Nations is baffling, not to speak of frustrating, and the use of the veto to prevent help is absolutely shameful. As mentioned above, the lot of official refugees can be considerably better than that of their internal counterparts. Examples of this would be the camps run by the Salesian James Somers àt Malindza and Ndzivane, Swaziland, from the late nineteen seventies to the mid nineteen nineties. Great concern was shown in these places for refugees who had fled the civil war in Mozambique. I recall that I was in Malindza one Easter and Fr Somers was striving to ensure that each family would be supplied with some oranges – so they would know it was Easter. As an added extra, this was a flourish, a tiny flourish.

Open house
Whether it be a case of refugees, asylum-seekers, or migrants, I believe that host countries should have a generous, welcoming policy towards them. Of course one understands if they are wary of real criminals entering their jurisdictions. As of now, however, the EU countries only consider people who are persecuted for political, religious or ethnic reasons as candidates for citizenship.

They are deaf to pleas because of economic or social deprivation from migrants who are seeking a better standard of living for themselves and their children. There is a fear that such people will take away jobs from locals. In Ireland, for example, that fear is palpable, because it is not too long ago since we ourselves suffered from acute unemployment and scurried for the green cards that would allow us to work legally in the US. We are the last ones that should create problems for expatriates. We ourselves travelled all over the world as economic refugees and owe so much to countries like the United States and Britain.

Generally people don't leave their homes easily unless driven by necessity, and very often they have the intention of returning one day. I once met a Sierra Leonean on his way back to Africa for the funeral of a relative. He was making good money in the US but was planning a return home eventually; he sorely missed the close family and community life of his African village.

That foreigners will be a drain on the economy mostly proves a myth. They usually contribute to the economies of their host countries and indeed are glad to do jobs that locals avoid.

Sadly, they are sometimes exploited and badly treated. It was so disappointing to hear a worker here in Ireland say recently, 'The employer treated us Brazilians like dogs.'

If we are realistic, we will see that the monochrome world is going. Not long ago to see a person of Afro origin on an Irish street was a rarity. Lenny Henry, the English comedian, was able to joke on one of our television shows that as he walked down Grafton Street people cried out, 'Hello Lenny!' because he was the only black man in Dublin. And, significantly, people saw the joke. But isn't our growing diversity much more stimulating? To see this we have to overcome our fear of the stranger who is not one of us (cf Mark 9:38-41).

It is painful that people are driven by circumstances from their homes and countries. If we think anyone does this without heartache, we are mistaken. In a sense, we never can or never do leave our places of origin. An Arab sage was reputed to have perceptively observed: 'In the town and streets where you grew up,

there will you always live, and there also will you die.'
And that's how it is.

* * *

Déjà vu

Eighteen forty eight
and with blurred eyes Pat looks
on Boston Common,
inconsolably
longing for Ballyhoge
and those he loves,
especially Maureen
whose face
he now accepts,
he'll never see again.

The date is nineteen ninety nine,
and Musa stands upon O'Connell Bridge,
yearning for Pendembu
(his thatched village
'mid the palms),
kind hearts,
and Salva, sadly gone,
as those passing
in stony silence
eye him – warily.
(J. O'H)

11: The Earth's Our Mother
(Women's Rightful Place)

Giving women their rightful place in the churches and society generally is one of the gravest social problems facing us today. Though it may be more acute in certain developing countries, it is a universal issue which, if neglected, will prove costly.

The first thing I have to say on this matter is that life experience, particularly in Africa and Latin America, has deepened my appreciation of women. Above all, I marvel at their strength in adversity. I recall Teresa in South America, the day after giving birth to a baby, copiously sweating as she scrubbed the laundry of the rich on a crude stone so that her family might survive. Indeed there were many Teresas. Then there were the mothers of Soweto, who during the bus boycotts in the struggle against apartheid, arose in the dark and walked for long hours to their domestic chores in the luxurious homes of white South Africans in Johannesburg. And at the end of the long trek back home in the evening, there was supper to cook. And male students, who had spent the day rioting against injustice, were languidly waiting to be served. Was the end of apartheid achieved primarily through the sacrifices of such valiant women? Nelson Mandela highly praises the contribution of women to the fight against apartheid in his moving autobiography, *Long Walk to Freedom*, chapter 28.[10] On the first page of that chapter he quotes Chief Albert Luthuli who, noting how women were defying the pass laws, said: 'When the women take an active part in the struggle, no power on earth can stop us from achieving freedom in our lifetime.'

It wasn't that the languid young men were lacking a sense of justice, but they obviously needed to think harder about what it meant. Women are taken for granted and domination is deeply rooted in the male psyche. Many males may not consciously

---

10. Nelson Mandela, *Long Walk to Freedom*, London: Little, Brown and Company, 1994, pp 206-209.

realise this and yet it is so. I have seen men who would be horrified to hear that they were chauvinist but fail to take women seriously, often showing this by treating them in a jocular fashion, as if they were children.

We need each other
We are all equally children of God. Genesis 1:27 reminds us of this when it says 'male and female God made them'. We need each other's gifts to keep this world healthy. Where would it be without the selfless, routine dedication of the women mentioned above, yet we need them in more high-profile positions too. Arguably our two best presidents here in Ireland have been female, Mary Robinson and Mary Mc Aleese. But if we look realistically at society, we would have to say that the male world seems reluctant to give women significant roles in public affairs. This is so even when men publicly proclaim their competence. Really, key appointments to positions of responsibility in church and state would be worth more than all the protestations.

I have to say that my own Catholic Church would appear to have problems in this respect. There are the documents but where are the appointments? Meanwhile women, who do most of the routine work in the church, often chafe under their exclusion from ministry – priesthood included – and various other forms of significant participation. Where ministry is concerned, tradition is invoked for passing them over. I believe, however, that we have to sift through tradition much more carefully to see what is doctrine and what is the result of social conditioning.

I recently did some work in Central Europe. A young woman impressed me there and I should like to relate something about her that reinforces what I have said about women elsewhere. Wheelchair bound, she was relating the story of her life in a small Christian community in Romania. She told of how she belatedly received First Holy Communion owing to the communist years of persecution and oppression. So happy was she that day, she wanted to stay in the church building forever. Even as she recalled this, the glow on her face and her smile told of her happiness. She wasn't cured of her disability on the occasion, yet she did receive more mobility, for which she was deliriously grateful. She went on to say that she lived in a room with another handicapped girl and between them they managed to survive. I didn't get the impression that any other person was helping them. 'But life is a huge struggle for us,' she concluded. There was silence.

I realise of course that the feminist issue is much more complex and extensive than the points I have made. My response to the problem is merely a personal one. I again recall an Indian woman in Ecuador. Her husband had just died and was about to be placed upon a table to be waked. What this simple woman said surprised me. 'No,' she protested, 'don't put him on the table. Put him on the ground. The Earth is our mother. We came from the Earth and we must return to the Earth. All life comes from her and all life must go back to her.' She was a fervent Christian yet the folk memory reached back through the mists, as the figure of the Pachamama, the Earth Mother, was overlaid with her Christian faith. There was the association of the beginnings of all life and endeavour with the female. It is a message of the utmost importance

* * *

Another View

(i) Copper Beech
Since I came back,
the copper beech has drawn
me aside, dipping its brush
into lenten leaf.

Occupant of many rooms,
how intimate its dealings
with light, shedding its weight
of shadow on the lawn.

(ii) Celie's Tale

'He beat me like he beat the children'

The farmhands' chopping
has left the windbreak
wounded; nobody minds.
In time the wooden flesh
will heal: trees feel no pain.
Celie makes herself wood,
knows that trees fear men.
(H.O'D)

Unquietly flows the Don
I met her at a meeting near Budapest. An elderly woman, she came to speak to me at the end of the gathering. A dedicated doctor stepped in to interpret. 'How old do you think this woman is?'
 'Late sixties or early seventies.'
 'She's ninety two!' Hard to credit.
Her husband was killed in the Battle of the Don on the Russian front during the Second World War, she told me, and showed me a faded photograph of a handsome young couple with three children, one a baby-in-arms. The man was in military uniform. Belatedly supported by the German army, 200,000 ill equipped Hungarians were slaughtered at the Don. She was left with the three young children. Such was her love for the young man that she vowed to God she would never marry again, would wait to be reunited with him in the hereafter. Through all of Hitler's war, through the bitter forty years of communist oppression, she supported her children and remained true to her vow. At the end of her sharing, since I couldn't converse with her directly in Hungarian, I gave her a hug. And she wept on my shoulder. I grasped, then, the immense suffering of the lost years – and the valour of this woman. (J.O'H)

12: The Search for Soulfulness
(Young People Taking Their Leave)

Why on earth should it be so? In our affluent western society young people have been taking their own lives in alarming numbers. A little village that I know in Ireland, which for obvious reasons will remain nameless, is agonisingly searching its soul for explanations as to why so many of its young people have chosen this path of no return. It is a question for all of us, especially those who live in wealthy communities. Parents who have lost children in this way are filled with anguish and often blame themselves, although experts tell us that very often they are not in the least blameworthy. Even the most loving and caring have had this tragedy befall them. We have to turn our gaze to the wider scene.

When I was a boy in rural Ireland during the thirties and forties, times were hard. People generally were struggling to survive but youth were not taking this way out. Many will have fond memories of their childhood in those years, though, in search of work, they were soon destined to take the emigrant boat to England, North America or Australia. I still feel in my soul the wound at having lost those dear companions to emigration: Dixie, Peter, Eddie, Paddy, Mary, Kitty, Ina ... Where are you now? What has life done to you? We now know that things were far from perfect in bygone days, following revelations of physical and sexual abuse in institutions and homes. I certainly do not wish to idealise those times. Nevertheless there was on the whole a strong sense of family, community and faith that are missing today, though we are materially much better off. Despite the hard times, there was a zest for life: somehow, when people struggle to live, it blunts a death-wish. In the little rural town where I grew up, I remember losing dear companions in accidents: one was electrocuted while climbing a pylon, and another fell through a glass-house and bled to death. But I cannot remember even one young person taking their own life. When I look back now, what stands out is the fun we had hurling in the Friar's Field, swimming in the Avonree, and dancing away long summer evenings on hastily erected platforms.

A gulf between
Though there is an alarmingly growing gap between haves and havenots in Ireland at the moment, there is no doubt that, as a nation, we have never been so well off. We are among the richest in the world. The famed Celtic tiger that weakened for a time seems to be healthily unsheathing its claws again. Yet it is not only Ireland that is opulent, the West and other industrialised areas of the world enjoy the same material well-being.

So why are are young people opting out of this material paradise? Could it be that it is precisely because it is primarily a material paradise? They walk through dazzling shopping malls, the great cathedrals of the consumer age, possessing spending money that boys and girls of my day could only have dreamed of. They want for nothing; there are goods to meet every possible need. The message of society comes over clearly: heaven is material possessions. But they have tasted this heaven and it is only ashes in the mouth. What then is there to live for? Life is being robbed of meaning.

Family and community, the real treasures, are breaking down. Though parents may do their best to cushion children from the shock of marital breakdown, the results are often (perhaps always) invidious for them. In the circumstances, young people often seek refuge elsewhere, so homelessness further complicates matters. The social dislocation resulting from the breakdown of the traditional family is having dire consequences. As I write, Ireland is being rocked by news of an incident where fourteen and fifteen-year-olds callously murdered some companions. The unimaginable is happening. Alcohol abuse, too, often exacerbates other ills; the lethal cocktail of alcohol and drugs can leave young people in such a crazed state that they don't know what they are doing. Children need stability and we have to be aware of the great upset in their lives when communities weaken and parents split.

THE SEARCH FOR SOULFULNESS

Obviously, when young people look at the international scene in the wake of 9/11, and now in that of 12/26, there is much to cause dismay, even terror. Add to this the acute pressures of various sorts: academic (the imperative to perform), emotional, psychological and it all adds up to a sea of troubles. Even having good trainers is not enough; if they don't bear the Nike swipe, the youthful wearer can be mocked by friends.

Waning spirituality

Religion also and religious practice are fading. Spirituality is thankfully surviving but where there is no practice this could eventually follow suit. A twenty-year-old German, on a visit to Ireland, expressed surprise at the existence of a spirituality among the young, saying that this was no longer generally so in Germany. So let us be warned; spirituality too can disappear. We must admit that historically we have had a dominating, clericalised and even oppressive church model, but there is no need to persist with such. It is high time that we implement the community model set forth by Vatican II. I hope and pray that we earnestly consider the implications of this new way of being church, because, if we do, it could become a more humble and better servant to the world. Young people might well 'tiptoe back to the church' (Emily O'Reilly) if it was of this kind. After all, it has wonderful news from Jesus to communicate; of himself he says: 'I am the way, the truth, and the life' (John 14:6) and 'I have come that they may have life and have it abundantly.' (John 10:10). Is a young person wondering which way to go in this world? Jesus provides a sure compass. Are they searching for the truth? He is the truth. Do they want to live life to the full? He will show them how.

* * *

Rest in Peace Louise

A voice on my answerphone brought me the news
'You remember Louise? She topped herself today.
Thought you should know. Sure she'd nothing to lose.'
Ah Louise, it's the world has lost – lost your charm.

I remember you returning from Bernadette's shrine
where your mother had brought you to pray about drugs.
The candle you carried like a victory sign
was taller than yourself, and you gave it to me.

We brought it to a convent. It burned there for days.
Often I've thought of your generous heart
and your eyes shining brighter than the candle's rays
with love for your mother, for your saint, for the world.

Ah Louise, is it true you had nothing to lose?
Your wee brother weeps, your mother's distraught
and the junkies lining up in the dealer's queues
have jettisoned dreams of escaping their lot.
(Brian Power)

13: I Ask Why People Are Hungry
(Religion and Politics)

Must religious people only busy themselves with incense and votive candles or retire to their sacristies? Where does religion sit with politics? Against the broad backdrop of justice and peace, this is a significant question. Politics is the dynamic way in which our whole secular life is organised. It concerns itself with health, labour, sport, finance, education, industry and commerce, communications, welfare and so forth. That is why we have government ministries to look after these areas. Must the churches be silent on such matters? This is precisely what the opponents of religion often understand by keeping out of politics. Of course this is absurd. Churches cannot opt out of politics, for to opt out of politics is to opt out of life.

Some time ago in a Sunday homily, I raised the issue of our Irish neutrality which seemed to me to be under threat from a creeping militarism that linked us to NATO and nuclear arms. Afterwards many people thanked me for raising the issue, saying they hadn't given it much thought. This dismayed me. Such a vital issue. But one irate parishioner told me: 'You are meddling in politics and are quite out of line!' He obviously felt that the church should have nothing to say on this matter of life and death.

But the foregoing was not just my experience. Dom Helder Camara, the last archbishop of Recife in Brazil and a great champion of the downtrodden famously said, 'If I feed the hungry, people say I am a saint. If I ask why people are hungry in the first place, they call me a communist!' But Camara never lost hope.

Politics and politics
Of course, as Sean O'Casey's Jenny Gogan might say, 'I don't know. I always say there's politics and politics in it.' There is politics in general and party politics. The churches and religions should not normally enter into party politics, unless a party that

is evil surfaces. The Nazi party that emerged under Hitler in the early thirties certainly needed to be condemned by name because of its lethal ideology. Indeed there were some people who did just that, among them two groups of extraordinarily courageous students. They called themselves The White Rose.[11] They were quickly rounded up. Three of the inspirational figures of the movement, Hans and Sophie Scholl, who were brother and sister, and Cristoph Probst were speedily convicted of treason and condemned to death. All witnesses attested to the awesome poise with which Hans and Sophie met their fate. They were beheaded on 22 February 1943.

If I might return again to the Latin American scene. Recent decades saw the emergence of liberation theology and basic Christian communities. Round these raged the debate of the church's involvement in politics; they were accused of being tinged with Marxist ideology. Now all theologies, liberation theology included, must be open to criticism. Liberation theologians, however, argue that their theology is rooted in the word of God – the Exodus story – and the experience of the downtrodden, not in the ideology of Marx. Having heard its chief exponent, Gustavo Gutierrez, speak at length, I am convinced it is so. As I myself see it, Jesus came to redeem us, not just from sin in some other-worldly sense, but from all the effects of sin – hunger, disease, poverty and oppression. So 'liberation' is at the heart of redemption. To call off true liberation theology would be like calling off the Redemption.

I find it noteworthy that, when Leonardo Boff went to Rome to defend his writings, he was accompanied by two cardinals, Arns and Lorscheider, men of great integrity. Two documents were issued from Rome during the 80s on the subject of liberation theology.[12] The second of these was much more positive

---

11. cf. Robert Ellsberg, *All Saints*, New York: Crossroad Publishing Company, 1997, pp 87-88.
12. *Instruction on Certain Aspects of the 'Theology of Liberation'* from the Congregation of the Doctrine of the Faith, 1984. *Instruction on Christian Freedom and Liberation* from the Congregation of the Doctrine of the Faith, 1986.

and conciliatory than the first. And John Paul II was quoted as saying that, correctly understood, liberation theology was 'not only opportune but useful and necessary.'[13] A criticism that can rightfully be made of liberation theology is that at the beginning its focus on the poor and oppressed was too narrow. In the intervening years this has been rectified. There are other forms of oppression and their theologies, which found inspiration in early liberation theology, are now also flourishing. Feminist and black theologies would be examples of these.

And as for basic Christian communities, now more commonly referred to worldwide as small Christian communities, they were never political cells, nor should they be. Of course in the Brazil of the 1970s, they were the only forums where citizens could express an opinion and people who primarily had a political concern went there. But once a semblance of democracy returned they found their forum elsewhere. In Central America some groups took the name 'Basic Ecclesial Communities', though they were purely political – theologically, they never were small Christian communities. These communities are faith experiences. Interestingly, where they exist, destructive sects have made no inroads; where they do not, they have created havoc. Incidentally, it emerged in the media that a report prepared for the Reagan White House by the CIA found that liberation theology and basic Christian communities were forces that forwarded democracy. This was not the report expected or wanted and, not surprisingly, was shelved. The administration was hoping for something that would support its policies in Central America, including its backing of the Contra rebels in Nicaragua.

The upshot of all this is that the church simply cannot opt out of politics properly understood; rather should gospel values guide it in making the political options most in line with the mind of Christ.

* * *

---

13. Catherine Pepininster ed., *John Paul II: Reflections from The Tablet*, London/New York: Burns & Oates, 2005, p 39.

A Hope-giving Review

The following is a quotation from the *Southern Cross*, August 10-15, 2005. It concerns a review of Professor Morozzo's book, *God First: The Life of Oscar A. Romero*, in *L'Osservatore Romano* and would, I feel, be true of all the leading exponents of liberation theology:

> The review highlighted Professor Morozzo's position that Archbishop Romero was not a communist, that he had not embraced a form of liberation theology so heavily focused on earthly realities that it ignored the spiritual and that he was always faithful to the teaching of the popes.

Hope is ...

Hope is an orientation of the spirit, an orientation of the heart.
It transcends the world that is immediately experienced
    and is anchored somewhere beyond its horizons.
Hope in this deep and powerful sense is not the same as joy
    that things are going well
        or willingness to invest in enterprises that are obviously
    headed for early success.
But rather an ability to work for something because it is good
    and not because it has a chance to succeed.
Hope is not the same thing as optimism.
It is not the conviction that something will turn out well
    but the certainty that something makes sense
    no matter how it turns out.
It is what gives strength to live
    and continually try new things,
        even in conditions that seem hopeless.

(*Vaclav Havel*)

14: A Gift to the World
(Africa's Sense of Community)

I have come to admire and love Africa and its peoples, so – I admit it – I am biased in their favour. Having had a relationship with Africa that goes back thirty-six years, I offer thoughts on that vast continent. I do this, bearing in mind that points relevant to Africa have already been made elsewhere in this work. Some Africans could find it invidious that an outsider, who can never fully grasp the complexity of their cultures, should express opinions about them. I am aware of my limitations in this respect, but I would respectfully suggest that an outsider can have a perspective that local people lack because of their emotional involvement in issues proper to them. Certain things become more apparent from a distance. Over the years my work there has taken me to all parts: north, south, east and west, so my views should not suffer from being too localised. In my travels I learned that listening with the utmost respect to what people had to say for themselves was of crucial importance. Without this no progress is possible.

Africa's contribution
Africa has a gift of incalculable worth to offer to much of our modern world, though the modern world may be surprised to hear this. I was once doing some work with a gathering of boys in their late teens in Cape Town during the apartheid era. They were in fact discussing apartheid. The group consisted of whites, so-called coloureds (mixed race) and blacks. A white lad, who was no bigot, said that blacks could not be blamed for being backward.

I quietly disagreed with what had been said and pointed out that developed societies might well have split the atom but had lost the skill of community. Among African societies, though menaced by western materialism and selfishness, family and community were still vital realities. People still knew that friendship was the earth's great treasure, not money, power or fleeting fame. A life that looks only to wealth, power or fame for sustenance will probably end up greatly diminished. So in the area that most matters – how to relate to our fellow humans – Africans have much to teach us. Technocrats can tell us how to make profits, but not necessarily how to conduct our lives.

Africans too are generally religious: they have a sense of the transcendent. I recall that, while teaching in an African high school, the question of God's existence came up for discussion. One lad ventured the opinion that there was no God. I'm afraid the others laughed him out of court as though this was the most stupid thing they had ever heard. There is no doubt but that the African sense of family and community is being enhanced by religious belief of whatever genre.

Owing to the menace of materialism mentioned above, Africans will have to be on guard if they are to preserve their way of life. It is also true that the sense of community often does not extend beyond family and the ethnic group to which they belong. There can be even deep-seated enmity between neighbouring tribes, which is a severe constraint upon something so valuable. Religions such as Christianity and Islam can make a positive contribution towards the solution of this problem since they transcend boundaries of tribe and nation. Christianity, for example, teaches an unconditional love of all persons, even enemies. Apart from a few troubled spots, I have found that relations between Muslims and Christians are good over much of the continent, so they would do well to join forces in pushing out the boundaries of acceptance and cohesion.

To the peoples of Africa we owe a deep debt of gratitude for keeping the lamp of community alight. It could be that the continent will give back its soul to the developed world.

Corrupt leaders
In general African nations have not been blessed in their politicians. Notable exceptions would be Nelson Mandela, Julius Nyerere and Leopold Senghor. Far too many have got to power so

as to enrich themselves and their cronies, usually of the same ethnic group. They are no patriots, less still statesmen. In reality they are criminals. Even some of the most promising only stop the gravy train long enough to get on, as Desmond Tutu tellingly put it. Autocrats, such as the late Mobutu, can pillage their countries while the world stands by; as long as trade flourishes many democracies turn a blind eye. This is simply reprehensible. We are badly in need of a World Court of Justice to which all nations, however powerful, submit. The principle of not interfering in the affairs of nations is thoroughly outworn because, in the end, we all rise or fall together.

The colonial period did of course spoil Africa in terms of its own autonomous development – remember the drowning fish! Indeed this development stood still as local peoples were reduced to a state of futile dependency. How would matters have progressed without this interference? We can only guess. Undoubtedly there would have been centuries of painful progress just as we have had in, say, Europe. One of the most harmful things that the colonials did was to draw frontiers dividing people of the same ethnic groups who should have remained together. The knotty problem created affects Africa to this day. I asked a learned African friend what he felt could be done about this. He believes that at this stage nothing can be done about boundaries but that a federal set-up within countries would be the most effective form of governance. If, however, people of the same ethnic groups can relate well across national frontiers, it could be a help rather than a hindrance in fostering good international relations.

From what I have written, it will be obvious that Africa needs the world, but not as badly, I think, as the world needs Africa.

* * *

Reaching out
(Story told by a man in a Kenyan small Christian community.)

Long, long ago a tribe of people lived on our land called the Jumas. These Jumas had very large heads. So large that, when they fell over, they could not get up. Like a beetle that gets turned on its back and then thrashes the air with its spindly legs and goes nowhere. If another Juma didn't come along and lift up the fallen one, it would mean death for the unlucky person – the same as the beetle. Sometimes, when Jumas fell over, there was no one to raise them up so they died. The result was that they began to get less and less in number and decided to go live underground – I suppose they couldn't fall over down there – and our people, the Kikuyus came to live on their land.[14]

---

14. James O'Halloran SDB, *Small Christian Communities, Vision and Practicalities*, Dublin: The Columba Press, 2002, p 64.

15: The Non-violent Alternative
(Active Non-violence)

It is hard to ignore figures like Martin Luther King and Gandhi who achieved so much through active non-violence; the non-violent alternative, however, can be summarily dismissed by the advocates of force. As we look at the world in 2005 with the messy aftermath of a war in Iraq, genocide threatened in Darfur, mayhem in the Middle East and so forth, it is obvious that active non-violence has not attracted a vast following. Nevertheless a look at the Gandhian approach would in the circumstances be timely.

Regarding the non-violent approach, the first myth that needs dispelling is that it means we do nothing. Quite the contrary. Every measure that is non-violent may be employed. Even if it is illegal? Nations have become great because there were good people who refused to obey bad laws. In the build up to independence, the people of the United States refused to pay taxes imposed by law because they had no representation at Westminster. 'No taxation without representation!' was the legitimate cry. Had the German people risen up to oppose the Nazis' 'legal' extermination of six million Jews, could Hitler have got away with it?

The non-violent methods are various. In the early nineteen sixties, Martin Luther King rallied 100,000 mostly Afro Americans in Washington DC to march on Congress and demand civil rights. Remedying legislation soon followed. Dan Berrigan and his associates in the peace movement, again in the United States, forced their way into a military installation and put a nuclear missile out of commission. I heard him later declare that this was the first act of unilateral nuclear disarmament in history and he called upon the Russians to respond. Rosa Parks simply refused to give up her seat on a bus. And Gandhi just asked the Indian people to produce their own salt and not buy the salt which the colonists provided. This was because the colonists had a monopoly on the sale of salt and made huge profits from the same. So Gandhi's clever stratagem proved economically crippling for them. Such are the methods employed. They deface property in certain circumstances but do no physical violence to the sacredness of the human person. The results were: civil rights won by Afro-Americans, India liberated, lives saved ...

And then there was the fall of communism, one of the greatest tyrannies the world has ever known. This great revolution was for the most part a peaceful, 'velvet' revolution. People power or people pouring spontaneously on to the streets to cry 'Enough!' brought down one violent and corrupt government after another. Records, of course, must give great credit to Mikhael Gorbachev who recognised that you can't roll back the flood of history and refused to call out the tanks as the Berlin Wall crumbled. For me, he was one of the greatest men of the twentieth century. In the endeavour to overcome communism, I regard his recipe for a stable world – social democracy – as ultimately the only viable option. Pope John Paul II was no slouch in bringing down communism either; the support he gave Solidarity in Poland was crucial. Gorbachev acknowledged that the overthrow of communism would not have happened without him. People power overthrew the Marcos regime in the Philippines. Intriguing also is how lay people are making their voices heard in the church and affecting decision-making, as happened in Boston. A cardinal decided to resign there as a result of lay protests regarding the mishandling of sex abuse scandals.

Not simple

Having opted for active non-violence myself, I must confess that implementing it is not without imponderables. If someone were to attack me or a friend, what would I do? Given the present crisis in Darfur where people are being killed with the connivance of their own government, who should be defending them, what action can be taken? In other words can we just stand by and watch people being attacked and killed? I don't think so but this doesn't mean that we ourselves attack and kill indiscriminately. I recently saw a flare-up at a sports event and some hefty punches were being thrown. One man just caught his assailant and so re-

THE NON-VIOLENT ALTERNATIVE

strained him that he was able to protect himself while the other calmed down. Regarding Darfur, other nations should intervene, under the auspices of the United Nations only and preserve the peace. The intention is that they go in to preserve the peace, keep opponents apart, restrain them from violence but not to maim or kill. When Australia, backed logistically by the United States, went into East Timor in 1999, they enforced the United Nations mandate and saved the people from genocide at the hands of militias masterminded by Indonesia.

The emphasis in East Timor was on restraint and peace-keeping and these worked. This of course was not the emphasis in Iraq and now we are mired in a conflict to which no one can see an end. Conflict is messy and it could be that in the examples given people would be injured or lose their lives. But that was never the intention. Ours is not a perfect world.

Though no system works perfectly on this planet, there can be no doubt but that the non-violent alternative is preferable to violence. A sad fact is that the proponents of this noble method often suffer jailing, violence or are themselves killed. Gandhi, Luther King, Brother Roger Schultz, and many others, male and female, had their wounds to show.

* * *

Christ Showing His Wounds
(stained glass, 14th-15th century, Hunt Museum)

like a footballer after the match
drawing up his trouser leg
to indicate where the kick has been given –
that bruising there a badge of having suffered
for the parish and proud to have done so.
(H.O'D)

Mayday[15]

(The following is a story taken from my novel *Remember José Inga!* which shows the power of active non-violence. It is of course fictional yet the core facts are true. How José Inga died is a dramatic tale and the following is some of the fallout from the event. Fr Fernando in this story was Inga's pastor and he was also pastor to the group taking part in the May Day demonstration that was in protest at a series of grievances.)

The first of May dawned gloriously. There was a distinct feeling in the air that dry weather had come and the rains had passed. Even the little breezes of summer blew spasmodically. As agreeable weather continued, these breezes would, quite unexpectedly at times, create small eddies of dust that were the tame and diminutive relatives of the fearsome twisters that erupted in other parts of the world.

Padre Fernando's group assembled in Colegio Domingo Savio not far from the route of the parade. He reminded them that they would walk in total silence and would not become involved in any kind of disturbance. In a reverent voice Marcelo Reyes now read a passage from 1 Peter 3: 'make a defence to anyone who calls you to account for the hope that is in you ...'

'Our hope,' said Alicia Córdova, 'is that a society where justice and peace reigns is achievable.'

'So let us march for that,' declared Jorge Correa. And the group set out with banner and placards held high to take their place in the parade.

All along the Avenida 12 de Octubre groups were assembling under their banners: socialists, communists, trade unions ... There were various stripes of communists: Maoist, Stalinist, Marxist-Leninist and Trotskyite. The 'Trots' were already in a polemic with a neighbouring band of Stalinists on recondite points of Marxist doctrine. They were sticklers for purity of doctrine and argued interminably about this in an effort to get things

---

15. James O'Halloran, *Remember José Inga,* Dublin: The Columba Press, 2004, pp 87-93.

straight. The problem was that, because of all the talk, there was no room for action.

Into this red sea the Santa Rosa Youth Movement inserted themselves specifically as a band of Christians. All the groups were so noisily taken up with their own preparations that they did not pay much attention to them. The odd person would read their placards with some puzzlement but no seeming hostility. After all, despite the political hoo-ha, many of them were ardent devotees of St Cajetan, St Francis, La Madonna de los Andes, Jesus de Gran Poder ... There were also of course some hard-boiled lefties. It was a motley human mass.

The banner carried ahead of the Christian group had the caption: JUSTICE IS THE NEW NAME FOR PEACE (Pope Paul VI). There was also a portrait of Paul. Other placards proclaimed, WAGES UP PRICES DOWN ... SOLUTIONS NOT OPPRESSION ... BLESSED ARE THOSE WHO HUNGER FOR JUSTICE ... and, most interestingly, REMEMBER JOSÉ INGA! beneath a drawing of José. His name and effigy were also prominent among the placards of other groups but for the youth of Santa Rosa he was one of their own. José Inga had indeed risen from the dead and was crying out for justice from the hearts of the people in this demonstration.

All around groups were starting up the chanting of their slogans, rather like an orchestra warming up for a symphony. *'El pueblo unido jamás será vencido!* The people united will never be defeated!' Were they aware of what they were saying? Or was it an empty ritualistic chant, rather like the 'Four legs good, two legs bad' of the George Orwell animal story? The placard of the Christians, WAGES UP, PRICES DOWN, had already captured attention and various bands were crying out, *'Sueldos arriba, precios abajo!'* Some varied this by dividing into two choruses: the first would sing, 'Wages' and the second reply, 'up', and then the first, 'Prices', and the second, 'down', like monks at vespers.

A couple of ringleaders were going about whipping up emotions. They came to the quiet Christian group and decided to urge them on. One of them began shouting, 'The people united will never be defeated! The people united will never be defeated!' while furiously beating time with his arms. His verve met with a wall of silence. He dropped his arms and looked at them curiously. 'Are they dummies or something?' he asked his two companions. 'If they would only do something ... even dance.' The facetious Patricio Silva just couldn't hold, so he burst out laughing. All the youthful eyes were filled with silent amusement at the bewilderment of the men. But Patricio was unable to contain himself, 'No, señor, we're not dumb, just deaf.' Giving him wry looks, the men moved on.

Gradually the parade got moving, and slogans echoed and re-echoed throughout the whole stream of people. What a racket there was as they wended their way along streets of varying surfaces: cobbles, tightly fitting stones, or tarmac. Spectators, dressed in their sunny best, lined the route or looked down on the throng from Hispanic balconies with finely wrought black railings. The parade went through the colonial heart of San Diego with its gleaming white houses and undulating russet-tiled roofs. For a change, the participants occasionally burst into song – the Spanish version of the American Civil Rights anthem, *We Shall Overcome*.

The Santa Rosa Youth Movement attracted a lot of attention as it went by. Why weren't they shouting? Or singing? The onlookers diligently searched their banners and placards for a clue – which was the purpose of the exercise. They were Christians. What were they doing in this parade?

This was also the preoccupation of an interviewer from the key Radio Bolívar. 'Padre,' he asked, 'what in the name of God are you Christians doing here among all these lefties?'

'Look at our banner. The new name for peace is justice. We are here pleading for peace, but peace with justice, because there's no peace without justice. We can't hide away in the sacristy. We must bring our message to everyone. To do this, we have to get out on to the streets. Not just preach to the converted inside our churches.'

'But you have to admit that you keep some strange company.'

'So did Jesus Christ.'

Other interviewers and newspaper reporters followed and the group got ample coverage and the chance to get their concerns across. The Gandhian strategy was working like a dream. At one point Marcelo Reyes whispered to Fernando, 'That Gandhi and Martyr Luther King were smart men.' Fernando frequently said 'Martyr' instead of Martin.

'I'll fix you when we get home,' said Fernando.

'If we get home,' said Marcelo, reminding Fernando that the day was not without its dangers. Yet trouble seemed unlikely. Unfortunately, there were people with other ideas.

The planned route of the parade took the participants past the Plaza Principal, where the Presidential Palace stood, and on as far as Plaza Santo Domingo where it was due to disperse.

As the Santa Rosa youth drew near the Plaza Principal, the parade came to a halt. Word filtered back that there was trouble up ahead. Distant shouting and the firing of tear-gas could be heard. There were even shots that sounded ominously like gunfire. News came back that on reaching the Plaza Principal, instead of moving on, those marching had halted and hurled slogans and insults towards the dictator, López Reinoso, within the Presidential Palace. These were then swiftly backed up by missiles as some extreme leftists inflamed the marchers. Chaos resulted when the security forces hurled themselves upon them.

Back where the Santa Rosa group were, the parade was fast disintegrating and participants and onlookers swirled about in a maelstrom of fear, bravado and confusion. Even above the roar of the crowd the ominous and mournful wail of an ambulance siren could be heard, the customary herald of violence and death. 'What will we do now?' Jorge Correa, the coordinator of the Santa Rosa group for the occasion, asked of a passing marshal of the parade. 'The best thing you can do is create all the mayhem you can, smash windows, burn cars, beat up a few oligarchs if you can find any.' Jorge recognised the ideology – progress from anarchy. Some of his teachers had tried to instil it more diligently than they taught their geography or history. He recoiled from what now seemed to him its obvious futility.

The group had a quick consultation. They would not be part of this. Pancho Orozco disagreed and left them. They then separated themselves from the heart of this swirling mass, climbed down a steep grassy slope and found themselves on an empty street. There they reassembled in an orderly fashion and commenced the march back to base, Colegio Domingo Savio.

Suddenly, they saw a line of helmeted, olive-green soldiers barring their way at the end of the street. The officer gave an order. They sank to one knee, rifles at the ready. What to do? The group marched steadily towards them, though fear gripped their hearts. Nearer and nearer they came. The officer and his men looked at them. They were coming in silence. Their banner read, The new name for peace is justice. They were not cursing, hurling insults or throwing missiles as students usually did. The officer was utterly baffled. The troops were just awaiting the order, Fire! Then Alberto, a tall gangly lad, surprised everyone by holding up a white handkerchief and advancing upon the soldiers. The officer gave an order. The soldiers held their fire. Alberto spoke with the officer. It transpired later that he told him they were a non-violent Christian group, demonstrating in peace for justice. Amazingly, the officer then gave another order and the line of soldiers parted 'like the Red Sea', as someone later described it, allowing them through.

But their troubles were not over. Having passed the soldiers, they were going down a steep cobbled street. At an intersection, they heard the roar of a revving engine. On another intersection to their right they saw the ugly and fearsome *trucutú*, the armoured vehicle used for riot control. It's the *trucutú*! they called out in unison and continued on their way down. The problem was that those in the *trucutú* had also seen them. In a matter of moments, there it was confronting them at the next intersection, squat and threatening, its cannons trained upon them. Again they approached inexorably, the guns moved to get them more accurately in their sights. They awaited breathlessly to be hurled over and dyed an irremovable red, for identification, by the force of jets of liquid fired from the cannons. Once more there was the inexplicable pause. Like the soldiers, these police seemed baffled by this group.

Realising that things were on a knife-edge, the intrepid Alberto again hurried forward with his white handkerchief. He spoke through a slit in the machine to the inmates. There was an eternal moment of silent, yet screaming, tension. Then, inexplicably, the monster reversed on to a nearby street and allowed them through.

The group could hardly believe what was happening. They now had tangible proof of the power of silence and the force of active non-violence. They had prevailed over the almighty arms of the oppressor. They had won. So full were their hearts of exaltation that they burst into song:

We shall overcome,
We shall overcome,
We shall overcome one day.
Oh deep in my heart,
I do believe,
We shall overcome one day.

Seeing their placards, a little man in hat and poncho approached Fernando. 'Padre, I knew José Inga well,' he announced proudly.

'Tell me about him,' replied the priest.

16: Father Forgive Them
(Forgiveness and Reconciliation)

No one pretends that forgiveness and reconciliation are easy. In certain personal and social situations they can seem almost impossible yet, without efforts to achieve them, justice and peace become mere willow-the-wisps.

Regarding them I should like to recall an incident that happened at Stanstead Airport. I was waiting to check in on Ryanair 285 to Dublin. Directly behind me there were two Dublin girls and I could not but overhear their conversation. They were returning home following a weekend in the English capital.

'Darren says he loves me,' announced one in that plaintive Dublin voice that suggested infinite patience with human frailty.

'Dat weirdo!' responded the other in alarm. 'Yer not havin' anthing to do wi' him ever again, are ya, ya headbanger?'

'Ah I dunno. He asked me to forgive him.'

'Janey, after all dat he done, yer not goin' to, are ya?'

'If ya love someone, ya have to forgive him every time he asks. Ya know wha' I mean? Ya can't be f***in' countin'!'

I'm not sure about the wisdom of the girl's getting mixed up with Darren again, but regarding forgiveness she was spot on. Indeed, without the 'embroidery', a Man said much the same thing long ago in the gospel (cf Luke 17:1-4).

There is a significant difference between forgiveness and reconciliation. No matter how bad or angry I feel, I can decide in my mind to forgive. Indeed we learn from the reference to the gospel just given that there must be no limit to the times we forgive. We are all a mixture of saint and sinner and because it is so, we offend one another, sometimes without meaning to.

Reconciliation, however, involves the healing of psychological wounds and that takes time. I can decide in my mind to forgive and this can be a good – even heroic – first step. I may have to be patient with my scarred feelings, however, as they lag behind my decision, even though I am disposed for reconciliation. The initial phase may have to be simply a matter of peaceful coexistence and then the offended parties can begin the painstaking work of building bridges of reconciliation.

Northern Ireland
As I write this, Northern Ireland is on my mind. If we wish to understand how intractable issues related to forgiveness and reconciliation can be, we need look no further. Given the depths of historic antagonisms, a person can only view the future with apprehension. We still have to get to the point of peaceful coexistence from which bridge-building can begin.

True, there have been significant gains in recent years. Despite sporadic criminal violence on both sides of the Unionist/Nationalist divide, the ceasefire holds. Also, a fostering of relationships between the opposing forces has already begun humbly at the grassroots and is producing small yet heartening results. It was largely the work of lesser officials. We seemed to be on the verge of a historic solution in December 2004. People held their breath. Then, as on so many previous occasions, hopes were dashed at the last minute. Then we had the Northern Bank Robbery and the brutal murder of Robert McCartney which cast a dark shadow on the IRA and Sinn Féin. The result of all this is that the minds of the antagonists have been powerfully concentrated and the only way forward is perfectly clear: the IRA must give up their weapons, fold their tents, and go away; Unionists (including the DUP) and Nationalists have to share power as outlined in the Good Friday Agreement and factions on both sides must have done with criminality. We live in hope.

Stop press! As I write, the IRA have made their statement of 28 July (2005), declaring an end to their campaign and the decommissioning of all their weapons. Again, we keep our fingers crossed.

Whether it be a nation or individuals, for wrongs to be righted they must somehow be faced up to and acknowledged. That the boil be lanced is a psychological imperative. The Truth and Reconciliation Commission in South Africa, headed by Archbishop

Desmond Tutu, was a splendid example of this. So harrowing were the deeds revealed, that Desmond Tutu broke down in tears on one occasion during the hearings but the process was therapeutic and the outcome salutary. There are those who believe that some of the accused revealed everything simply to escape prison and that they had no remorse. But they did have to reveal everything. And they were publicly shamed.

The lancing of the boil is as psychologically important for individuals as for states. An example, again from South Africa, will illustrate the point. It is not about an accused person, rather does it concern a victim who had to face up to her own woundedness. Susan was the name of the lady concerned and I had the honour of meeting her a few years ago. In 1967, during the struggle against apartheid, her husband was slowly and brutally murdered. As if this wasn't tragedy enough for one lifetime, her two sons and a nephew were shot during the students' uprising in Soweto, 1976. She herself suffered exile in Cuba and Tanzania and, in the course of this exile, had to battle tuberculosis. Gnawing homesickness eventually drove her back to South Africa and the graves of her loved ones. She was bitter. And who would deny that she had ample reason to be so? One day, however, she sat down and took stock. 'This hatred is a poison that is consuming me,' she thought, 'and the fathers and sisters are so good to me. Not all white people are bad. I can't go on like this. I must forgive and be reconciled.' And she forgave from her heart. Yet the wounds are still healing, slowly. Not only are there hidden psychological scars to mend: on her body physical scars resulting from torture are only all too evident. Ironically the man who killed her husband endured a lingering agonising death himself, from AIDS. Susan did not gloat; for him she had only prayers and compassion.

Forgiveness such as this is the cement of broken hearts, broken community and a broken world.

***

FATHER FORGIVE THEM

Omagh 1998

It was not that I didn't try
to commemorate that blast
but nothing I wrote could mirror
the horror
or dignify the murdered.
That's all I can find to add
to the mountain of revulsion.
(Brian Power)

PART TWO

Community

1: Barbarians at the Gates
(Community in Disarray)

A brutal guerrilla war drags on in Iraq, parts of Africa are in turmoil, the problem of the Middle East continues to fester and, of course, there were the unspeakable horrors of New York, Madrid and London where mass death was visited upon innocent people going unsuspectingly about their daily lives. Furthermore, the prevailing ideology of liberal, free-market capitalism is making a god of money, fracturing human relationships and breeding societies that are infected with individualism and selfishness. No doubt about it, at the outset of this third millennium there are strong indications that community is breaking down in the world.

Fortunately, some people are beginning to wake up to the situation, even though they realise that it is already late in the day.[16] It is not just that the barbarians are at the gates, they are already inside. Civilisation itself is in peril. In the United States, for example, there are a plethora of books pleading for the restoration of community. One such would be Robert Wuthnow's *Sharing the Journey: Support Groups and America's New Quest for Community* (New York: The Free Press). In the States there is a tradition of rugged individualism – the John Wayne syndrome – yet there is also the communitarian tradition of John Smith and the early New England settlers. People are now beginning to look more closely at the virtues of the latter.

Given this apocalyptic scenario, there is only one possible answer – to restore community. It is the ground of being for justice and peace, and everything we say about community in this section has a bearing on these. As already noted, life is about relationships, not power and money. Banks can collapse overnight, mighty politicians fall. Friendships are the real treasures; no wonder the Bible says: '... the person who has found a friend has

---

16. cf Michael J. Farrell, *National Catholic Reporter*, (Kansas City, USA), September 5, 1997, pp 25, 34.

found a treasure' (Sirach 5: 9-13). So the task of ending divisions is urgent. Where to start? In our own hearts. Community means right relationships with ourselves, God (or whatever gives meaning to our lives), every person and creation round about us. This is an all-encompassing vision that relates divine, human and creational communities in a bond of respect.

The restoration of community, then, begins in our own hearts. If there is division there, we are severely hindered in our efforts to foster cohesion in our homes, neighbourhoods and society at large. Apart from the individual heart, unity has to begin in our homes – above all, in our homes. Hence the wisdom of Joyce Kilmer when he writes:

And the only reason a road is good,
as every wanderer knows,
Is just because of the homes, the homes,
the homes to which it goes.
(Roofs)

Regarding right relationships with God, I'm aware, of course, that some people are unable to believe in God. Yet they can be in harmony with whatever it is that gives meaning to their lives (the word of God is written on all our hearts since creation). It is essential that there be something that gives meaning to our lives – love would be an example. I understand that it was those prisoners who grimly held on to something that gave meaning to their lives that were able to survive the horrors of Nazi concentration camps. I found that people in situations of oppression in South America were sustained by their Christian faith. Ideally we would be at peace with all our brothers and sisters on this planet and cherish our environment. As I said elsewhere, if we continue abusing the planet as we are doing, it will become uninhabitable for our children and grandchildren. All this is not easy. But the day we cease to dream is the day we die.

Implementing the vision
This is the vision: a wholesome relationship with ourselves, the Creator – or whatever is the source of meaning in our lives –

neighbours and the environment. How to realise this is the problem. One strategy that is yielding positive results is to foster small communities, Christian or other (in India small human communities are proving most helpful) of about ten people in an area and then encourage them to network with one another, so as to create a communion of communities. Community involves intimate relationships and this can only be achieved in reduced groups. But these can network with one another and bring a sense of community to a whole area, even to those who are only loosely associated with such groups. All are enveloped in their light.

A brief word of clarification about the small human communities in India. Their concern is for the betterment of society; they are civil groupings rather than religious; nevertheless, because of their praiseworthy objective, religious people gladly join and support them.

There are, of course, sociological differences between a group and a community. People in groups, though they may get on well together, do not necessarily feel the need to relate closely. Their purpose in being in the group could well be to gain some skill and relationships would not be a major consideration. Not so with communities. Relationships are of the essence. And relationships take time to build. Even communities are groups to start with and groups can be the first step on the road to forming small communities. I have noted that groups that persevere are those where relationships are the priority.

I do not point out this difference between groups and communities through a lack of appreciation for groups. It is simply a matter of mentioning a divergence that sociologists indicate. Indeed my own aspiration would be that small Christian communities would promote, and network with, other small Christian communities but also with groups or communities of all kinds, whether religious or civil, that are doing anything to build a better world. Not only is there a vision for the world in such an aspiration, there is also the practical orientation as to how it might be realised. That all these groups would network and support one another would be important. This, in fact, is the only sure way that society can be renewed. Reform can come from above; renewal only from the grassroots and reduced groups are vital to the renewal of society.

To conclude I reiterate, life is about relationships. How monumentally wrong Mrs Thatcher was when she said there was no such thing as society. Borrowing words from John McEnroe, we say: 'Margaret, you can't be serious!'

* * *

The Pelican[17]
Near the Pacific coastline shoals of tiny gleaming fishes gambolled and fed, blissfully unaware of the flock of pelicans which flapped along gently overhead in V formation, their eyes riveted on the steely waters below. Suddenly there was a glancing flash of silver near the crest of a wave and a pelican shot headlong upon its prey. The fish narrowly escaped the thrusting beak and scurried panic stricken beneath a rock, shaking a nebulous galaxy of gold in its wake.

The frustrated pelican rode the waves for a moment and then spread her wings to take flight. Pain yelled through her right wing. She gave a little cry of agony. Again she flapped her wings in a vain attempt to rise; once more there was the excruciating pain. Terrified she sank back into the water. Her recklessly courageous dive had broken the wing on the sharp edge of a wave.

Pitying the bird, I approached to help. With racing heart she swam away from the shore to the safety of deeper waters. Locked forever in some remote corner of her brain was the image of a boy wantonly shooting her partner, who had then floundered agonisingly in the sea but lay still at last as the water turned to crimson all around him.

For long hours she fought the swing of the ocean. The debilitating wing, however, took its toll and the tide gradually edged the ruffled bird, exhausted, on to the beach.

---

17. James O'Halloran, *The Least of These*, Dublin: The Columba Press, 1991, p 67.

As I gazed at the light-ochre evening reflected dreamlike in the vast canvas of the ocean, I sighted her once more, a tiny dot on an endless strand. Out of her element, she was plodding laboriously along.

While she forged relentlessly onward, it did not occur to me that she could have any particular destination in view. But far up the beach on a finger of sand left protruding into the Pacific by the receding tide, her companions stood huddled against the terrors of the encroaching night. It couldn't possibly be that she, a maimed pelican, was trying to reach them.

As the minutes passed though, I realised that to reach them was precisely what she wanted to do. I became totally absorbed as the little drama unfolded.

The bird inched along, blinded by pain, in a seemingly hopeless struggle against distance and darkness. Would she make it? How she must have felt like bedding down on the inviting sand and drifting away into forgetfulness. From time to time there were little cries of complaint against her fate. Gliding over the sands to join her friends would formerly have been a small matter. Nevertheless she persevered in her effort and, after what seemed an age, that perseverance was rewarded, for only a narrow channel of water and a small portion of beach separated her from her companions.

Gracefully she breasted the water and crossed over. At the channel's edge she paused, momentarily worn out by her long endeavour. She then covered the remaining yards. Despite the devouring pain, joy surged within her. On reaching her friends she gave a muffled cackle of greeting and contentment. But the silent flock promptly rose and flew away, leaving the stricken one to the engulfing darkness.

The Brendan Prayer
(St Brendan the Navigator)

Sun, glancing off ice,
gleaming on snow,
glistening on frost,
for you.

Wind, coolly caressing,
filling the sail,
impelling the craft,
for you.

Sea, singing sweet psalms,
hinting at sagas,
whispering of ghosts,
for you.

Fish, leaping of silver,
gliding of fin,
cascading of whale,
for you.

Wailing gulls,
soothing albatross,
fleeting swallows,
for you.

Clouds flying, billowing, forming
dragon, sheep-flock, precipice,
for you.

Glory of dark storm,
roar of great wave,
terror of lightning,
for you.

And at last –
Solid rock,
A welcoming hand,
and a quiet cove,
for you.[18]
(J. O'H)

---

[18]. James O'Halloran SDB, *The Brendan Book of Prayer for Small Groups*, Dublin: The Columba Press, p 6.

2: The Sweetness of Togetherness
(The Church as Communion)

What I am about to deal with is crucial for all the Christian churches. Indeed I believe that it is relevant for people of all religions and none, if they clothe what I am saying in their own language and see it in the light of whatever it is that gives meaning to their lives. As already mentioned, I come from a Catholic background, I am Irish, but I have the deepest respect for peoples of all creeds and none. I hope, then, that the reader will understand me, because we come from where we come from, yet all people of goodwill are on a search for the the same reality – the truth that sets us free.

In March 1994, I facilitated a workshop on small Christian communities in Nairobi. At the beginning the participants were sharing experiences of such communities and I found the anecdote of a young woman called Sylvia of particular interest. 'When I left school,' she informed us, 'I would say I had the faith. I lived on the outskirts of Nairobi and every Sunday travelled by bus to the centre of the city where I attended the Mass in the Holy Family Basilica. But the basilica was very big and I didn't know anyone much. I felt alone. In the pulpit the priest talked about love and community, yet somehow I didn't understand. Then going home one Sunday and feeling a bit depressed, I said to myself, "I don't have a spiritual friend in the whole world".'

This was the low point of Sylvia's narrative and what she was saying was truly sad, because none of us goes to heaven alone. We are saved through relationships. The Bible says that it is not good for us to be alone (cf Genesis 2:8). A person who cuts herself off from others is a human contradiction because, without one another, we could not even learn to be persons. Without the sunshine of love and the rain of acceptance, we cannot grow as persons. We couldn't talk, maybe not even walk.

Sylvia went on to say, however: 'Soon afterwards I came across a small Christian community in my area and became a member. With that, all changed. In the community I didn't simply hear about love, as in the basilica, I actually experienced it, tasted the sweetness of togetherness. And little by little I grew spiritually, gained new ideas, made good friends and was able to take part in work for my neighbourhood. I blossomed as a person. No longer am I the girl who travelled alone into Nairobi, was lost in the big church and returned home downcast.'

What Sylvia was experiencing, by the power of the Holy Spirit people are experiencing in thousands of such groups on every continent. Furthermore the Spirit who was at work at the grassroots also blew strongly on this theme at Vatican Council II (1962-65). Paragraph 4 in the *Dogmatic Constitution on the Church* says: '... the universal church is seen to be "a people brought into unity from the unity of the Father, Son and Holy Spirit".' These to me are among the most significant words of the twentieth century, with far reaching consequences for the church and the world. Also noteworthy is that the proposal of the church as communion in modern times has come from two sources: the World Council of Churches in Geneva and Vatican Council II. For years the World Council of Churches had done research on the church as the 'People of God', a model that emphasised the role of the laity. This research was made available to the participants in Vatican II. So, from two sources, Geneva and Rome, there flowed the model of church as communion in the image of the Father, Son and Holy Spirit.

In effect we are asked in the church to be community as the Trinity is community. This raises intriguing questions as to what kind of community the Trinity is. Just to choose a few challenging facts, the Trinity is a community where there is:

- intimate loving and sharing,
- full participation of the three members,
- absolute equality of persons,
- and outreach to the other.

How do we replicate this in the church? How do we order the church so that there is intimate loving and sharing, full and responsible participation of all the members (even in decision-making!), the understanding that all are fundamentally equal through baptism, and that all must show concern for others, especially the deprived and disadvantaged. Well, one important way in which it is already happening is through the development of small Christian communities that are multiplying in thousands on every continent. I have just returned from working in the Carpathian Basin and in Hungary where, for example, there are in excess of 10,000 such communities of varying origins. These communities are open to, and network with, one another thereby helping to make bigger entities, such as the parish, a communion of communities. This even though some members of these larger entities may, by choice, have only a loose connection with the communities. The witness of small communities can touch the lives of all.

Needless to say, it is not possible to implement the characteristics of the Trinitarian community, listed above, as effectively in a parish of thousands, or even in a gathering of a hundred, as in my small Dublin community of ten. Intimate loving and sharing, for example, could not be realised. Full participation of all the members would also be out; imagine trying to conduct a dialogue among a hundred people. I think I would prefer to be playing golf, erratic and dangerous to bystanders though my game may be. Most members would be left out of the discussion – a real problem when decisions are arrived at through dialogue and consensus as in the small communities.

Here we have been talking only church. But the church, above all, cannot be self-regarding but has to be concerned with building a better world. In Christian terms we would refer to this as the kingdom of God; a reality that I will reflect on later. Down the years my own vision has been expanded by the challenge from those of all creeds whom I have met. I now believe that we should encourage groups of all kinds, whether they be religious or civil, that are doing anything to make life better for people. I would have them support and network with one another and press the powers-that-be, political and other, in the cause of justice.

* * *

Spanish Point
These three –
darkness stirring,
wind, high as kite,
sea dumping sea

as one –
mindless excess,
a kind of divinity,
kisses blown.
(H.O'D)

Dialogue with the Bishop
I recently had a conversation, lasting about two hours, with a wonderful bishop who put to me some questions that really forced me to think. Let me record two of them:

Bishop: At the beginning of this new millennium what do you think the church should do?

Myself: Bishop, there is a county in my country, called Kerry, where people answer a question by asking another. What do you think is the purpose of the church?

Bishop: What do you mean by that? (This bishop was as cute as any Kerryman!)

Myself: The history of salvation from the beginning has been the story of a remnant who remained faithful to the covenant with God. Only a minority of the Jews chose to return from bondage in Babylon to Jerusalem and rebuild the temple. A minority who remain faithful has been a recurring theme. So do you think the church is meant to be a mass movement or rather is it about a remnant that remains faithful; a remnant, however, that is a leaven whose humble presence is crucial for the well-being of the whole world?

Bishop: I believe its purpose is to be a faithful remnant [he was decisive]. But let me return to my question and be specific. Suppose you were made bishop tomorrow [having got a glimpse of his appointments diary, I

	blanched at the mere thought of it] of a diocese with a million people, urban and rural with, let's say, 150 priests and 200 parishes. What would you do?
Myself:	I knew a diocese in South America where there was a million people and eleven priests ... I once heard a bishop in Brazil, Pedro Casaldáliga now retired, say: 'Every year I sit down with the priests and the people and we plan for the diocese together. The fact that I am a bishop doesn't put me above or below anyone. We are brothers and sisters in Christ. We all play our part in building up the community; I act as a friend, a guide, a resource, above all, as a unifier ... My authority consists in being a humble servant to the community. It is the community that is important. Others bring their gifts for the same purpose: some are good at music or working with youth; others are interested in liturgy or justice and peace and so on ... It's the community that is the body of Christ, not any one individual; the wisdom of the Spirit too resides in the whole community and that is why decisions must flow from dialogue within the community.' If I were made bishop of the diocese about which you speak, this is how I would proceed. I would search for a path in dialogue with the people of God.
Bishop:	Let's have a glass of wine and drink to that.

(J. O'H)

I Have to Listen

If I were a zealous person
like some in the gospel
I would say it is forbidden
for anyone to speak –
only I, the bishop, am allowed to speak.
No, I have to listen
to what the Spirit is saying
through God's people
and then analyse it with them
and together use it to build the church.
(Archbishop Oscar Romero)

3: Story of a Small Christian Community

The importance of the small Christian community to the vision we are sharing will now have become clear. Hence it could be helpful to give the story of one such community. I choose my Dublin group. I do so, not because it has necessarily been the best or most exciting community I have known, but because I have been a member of it for twenty three years.

It started in 1982. There was a summer project for children and some of the teenagers involved in running that successful enterprise built up a camaraderie and felt they would like to go on meeting as a group when the project had finished. A Salesian seminarist put them in contact with myself because he knew I had been involved with small Christian communities for a considerable time and might be able to help.

Following discussions about its feasibility, a group got under way. The intention was that it be a Christian community. In Latin America and Africa, where I had been working, you could start directly on forming a small Christian community, because there was a great sense of community in those places. Even in the Ireland of the early eighties it was not quite so. This was something I had to learn and I also had to learn that a more softly, softly approach was called for. In other words, a sense of process was required.

The group was composed of about fifteen young people – somewhat too numerous for a small Christian community – and there was a reticence, but not hostility, among them towards religion. The result was maximum discussions about teenage issues (drink, drugs, relationships ...) and a minimum of prayer. It wasn't that there was little prayer, really there was none to start with. Then we began tentatively to end the gatherings with the Lord's Prayer. And after a time, someone noted one evening that there was a 'mighty' passage in scripture regarding the subject we had been discussing. It was duly read and considered. And so, almost imperceptibly, prayer and Bible-sharing crept in. Indeed, after a few years, that same group could place a candle in a sacred space in the middle of the floor, put out the lights and gather round to pray deeply for an hour or more.

As a result of the Bible-sharing and prayer, the members developed a hunger for knowledge of God and, though many of them were just beginning their working lives, they nevertheless did courses in theology and related subjects – and paid for them out of their own pockets.

And so it went. There were well attended weekly meetings – teenagers love meetings – and matters progressed. I believe that this was the moment when indelible impressions were left regarding the value of Christianity and community.

Action
Coming, as I did, out of a Latin American experience of the 1970s, I was keen on, and vocal about, issues of justice. I was insistent on the matter with the group. They, however, were not in the same place as myself. As one member put it, 'I believe I should try to be helpful at home, at work and in the neighbourhood, but I don't feel able to go out on the barricades to fight for justice.' So from the beginning there was the realisation of the imperative of being helpful and bringing Christian values to the home, places of employment and neighbourhoods; with time, however, the members also 'got out on the barricades'. Some of them, for instance, became deeply involved in the Ogoni issue at the time Ken Saro Wiwa was murdered, by protesting outside the Nigerian Embassy and Shell petrol stations. The Northern Ireland issue also aroused on-going concern. When the ceasefire broke down, the community contacted all the protagonists urging them to restore it and a young couple with their infant daughter travelled to Belfast to join a demonstration for peace. On the way, their train was stoned.

I also recall that there was much discussion in the eighties about prayer and action, how these had to be kept together. Prayer without action was not satisfactory on the one hand, while action that wasn't backed by prayer left much to be desired on the other. Then one night Dolores said, 'Look, I think this argument is futile. If I am truly a Christian, I will both pray and reach out. Birds fly, because their nature is to do so; Christians pray and reach out to others, for that is what genuine Christians automatically do.' I remember thinking to myself: 'My God, Dolores has resolved the faith-and-works issue of Martin Luther!'

The social side was also important to the community. All life's significant landmarks were duly celebrated and together they went on outings, holidays, pilgrimages, retreats and so forth. On one memorable occasion they were marooned on a sandbank in the Shannon and had to be rescued. We'll not go into whether the fault lay with the helmsman or those who distracted him from his task; the controversy rages to this day!

And so the story of our group continued more or less smoothly until Ciara was born. Little did we realise the shake-up the Holy Spirit was going to give us through the birth of Ciara. And you couldn't possibly have expected it because Ciara was a placid child and slept blissfully through our meetings. Gemma and Ger, two of our members, married and had the baby Ciara. They wanted to attend the meetings still but could not leave Ciara at home, so they brought the baby in her pram.

In due course various other members married and had children and still carried on trying to juggle between attention to the babies and fidelity to the community. It all became very difficult and we went though a lean period not knowing quite how to cope. One thing of which we were always convinced was that the family had to come first. What had really happened of course was that we had outgrown the teenage group model on which we had operated successfully for so long. A new model was called for but the Spirit, in whom we never lost confidence, left us to struggle. We had to be patient. Then the chrysalis evolved into a butterfly and a new model gradually emerged.

Family church

What we now have is a family-church model. We come together on the first Sunday of each month, celebrate the eucharist, pray, and reflect on the scriptures together. The little ones are taken out during the homily for a Sunday-school type of session, while the bigger children and their parents remain in church. The eucharist is children friendly and, as a result, we've had them pestering their parents as to when we're having the next Mass. Quite a turn-up for the books! The ceremony is of course followed by refreshments and the adults get a chance to chat while the youngsters gulp down their goodies and dash off to football or whatever. One little girl, I am told, refers to our eucharist as 'the biscuit Mass'. (I'm not quite sure what to think of that!) It does seem to bear out what the founder of my Salesian Congregation, St John Bosco, once said: 'The way to a child's heart is through their tummy.' On a special occasion we've had a barbecue and a bouncy castle. I see all this as making Christ known and imparting a love of community through experience – the only valid form of passing on the faith or evangelising.

I have been encouraging families to have a home meeting, apart from the monthly Sunday session, to pray and share the scriptures together and maybe invite in a few neighbours. This would mean that other groups would radiate from the main community. If we really wish to help our children, it is not enough to rely on family and small community, supremely important though these may be; we will be concerned for the wholesomeness of the total environment. Hence the value of letting the light shine. I don't know if anyone has taken up my suggestion about the home session so far but one member said, 'Keep on reminding us. Even if nothing seems to be happening, it's important we hear the message.'

The family-church community has always been associated with our Salesian house. However, our local parish has 30,000 members. Down the years it has been a traditional parish, due to some extent to the age profile of priests and people. Nevertheless the members of the small community, though themselves a community model of church, have always striven to reach out to the parish by attending services, acting in ministerial roles, being on councils, taking up bucket collections and so on. As of now the parish is establishing a parish pastoral council and is expressing an interest in small groups. Two of our members are on the pastoral council and five are eucharistic ministers. Given these stirrings, it seems that the parish will be more a home to communities such as ourselves in the future.

Out of the mouths ...

I return to Ciara to relate a concluding story. We were celebrating a Mass in the house of her parents, Ger and Gemma. Ciara and Niamh, the second baby in our community, were looking on in wonder at me standing in vestments. The following conversation occurred between Ciara, who could not have been more that two at the time, and Gemma her mother:

Ciara: 'Mummy, why is Jim dressed like that.'
Gemma: 'He's going to say Mass.'
Ciara: 'Is this a church?'
Gemma: 'No, this is not a church.'
Ciara: 'What is a church?'

Gemma looked patiently up to heaven while those present were bemused by the growing polemic.

Gemma: 'A church is a place where Jesus lives.'
Ciara: 'But Jesus lives here.'
Gemma: 'Yes, Jesus lives here.'
Ciara: 'Then this is a church, isn't it?'
Game, set and match!

* * *

Doctor and Mother
(For Peggy)

Eyes glazed but resolute you outlined
a course I could not sanction or oppose.
Words cannot enshrine your heroic resolve
you who were skilled in medical art
warm and resourceful paediatrician
knowing all about what drugs
might ease the pain of your wasting
from a disease whose name I've forgotten.
You I have never forgotten.
Your decision to reject the numbing effects
of opiates so that your children might
remember you as an attentive mother
alert for their need to love
wakeful and embracing – that decision
much as I longed to see your suffering banished
even as it pierced my heart with horror
stamped on my mind a lasting admiration.
(Brian Power)

4: *Three Dancers One Dance*
(The Spirituality of Small Christian Community)

You don't think up a spirituality and then impose it on small Christian communities. What is spirituality anyway? There was even a time when I wondered if there was such a thing; it seemed so close to theology applied with imagination and sensitivity. I have shared throughout the world on the subject of small Christian communities in accordance with my experience of their workings in neighbourhoods, mission stations and parishes. The approach was purely pastoral. But sometimes I would be thrown – and forced to think – by questions like, 'What is the theology of small Christian communities?' or 'What is their spirituality?' Usually these queries were put by academics. The general run of people were busy 'doing' small Christian communities and not too much time was given to philosophising about them. I realised, however, that such questions had to be treated with respect and that I had to do some further thinking.

I was already convinced by this time that spirituality, and indeed theology, needed to be earthed in reality. When you had a body of experience on which to reflect, the resulting conclusions about spirituality would be more assured. And there was such a corpus of experience to be found among the small Christian communities throughout the world. Understanding spirituality, therefore, to be a lived experience of faith, I set about consulting members of the communities in various parts of the world, not least those of my own Dublin group. What were the elements that moved them in their relationships with God, self, brothers and sisters, and all creation? I share the findings with the reader.

Like the Trinity
Christopher Mwoleka is a community member that I must mention by name. He is now deceased but I found he gave me huge inspiration. He had an insight that truly impressed me. It is obvious really yet it is easy to miss the obvious. Mwoleka looked at

his small Christian community in Tanzania and said, 'We are a dozen [or whatever] distinct and estimable persons here, yet through our intimate loving and sharing we are one. We are like the Trinity: three distinct persons but one God or one community. God is community.' This is a straightforward insight. Nevertheless as we saw in our previous piece, 'The Sweetness of Togetherness', it has tremendous consequences. The consciousness of this rootedness of small Christian communities in the Trinity would be the hallmark of their spirituality.

Mwoleka was a bishop who lived in an Ujamaa village in the same conditions as the other villagers. He was a different kind of bishop though – no palace for him, no dreaming spires. You may recall that the outstanding President Julius Nyrere of Tanzania promoted Ujamaa ('togetherness') villages where people could live and farm in community. Another reason for doing this was to gather people in convenient centres where services such as health and education could be more easily provided. If people were thinly scattered, it made this difficult.

Mwoleka thought this was a worthy scheme, so he himself lived and farmed in such a village. In the evenings he would sit and chat and smoke his pipe (naughty!) with other farmers and fellow community members. Regarding his insight that small Christian communities are rooted in the unity of Father, Son, and Holy Spirit, I have found no one who would disagree. As Tanzanian Christians aptly put it: 'There are three dancers but only one dance.'

Christ and the Spirit

As I chatted, without a pipe, but with small Christian community members in various places about Christ, I noted something special. Yes, they understood that they were body of Christ and that faith in him was the bedrock of their communities. What really struck me though was the warmth of their relationship with him. It was almost as if he were another member present in the room. He was a 'buddy', a 'mate', a 'chum', a 'soul friend' (*anam chara*) or 'compadre', depending on where you were in the world. His was the empty chair at the table. If a gleaming white dove were to flutter down and land on the back of such a chair, as I once saw in a theatrical production, you'd know it was the Spirit of Jesus.

And talking about the Spirit, there is a sensitivity to the workings of the Spirit in the small communities that would put you in mind of the Acts of the Apostles, which might as well be called the Acts of the Holy Spirit (cf Acts 15:28). With the help of the Spirit the early followers of Christ discerned their every move; in the groups it tends to be the same. This is surely a welcome development. While growing up, I didn't think too much about the Spirit. Frankly, the Spirit was a bird. And I doubt if I was unique in thinking like that.

Being rooted in the Trinity, embraced by Jesus, and inspired by the Spirit gives participants in the groups a profound sense of being permeated with the love of God, God who *is* love (1 John 4:8). We belong to God. God holds us in the palm of his hand. Even before we were born or could begin to love God, God first loved us (cf John 15:12). And this love of God is without conditions. The Lord doesn't say: 'I will love you but only if you are good.' Whether we are good or bad, God still loves us and works for our salvation. God is love and cannot do otherwise. God's love for us is something that we have to know, not just in the head but in the heart or, more graphically, in the gut.

At a session in Zimbabwe, we were sharing on John 17:20-26. Following the session a little sister approached me. 'Jim,' she began, 'I was really impressed by those words of Jesus, "I pray not only for them [the apostles], but also for those who believe in me because of their message." I am among those who believe in his message because of the apostles. Jesus was praying for me at that moment! The poor soul, he was going out to die and he prayed for me. I felt like crying. I work as a chaplain in the mission hospital. Many people there are dying of AIDS ... young people ... some of them relatives ... and they fear death. Now I'm going to be able to say to them, don't be afraid. Look here in the gospel; Jesus prayed for you. There's no need to be afraid.' That sister had grasped God's immense love for her and her neighbour.

When people are conscious of this love, it can change the whole way they see life. Take human love. They will perceive its roots deep in the mystery of the love of Father, Son and Holy Spirit. They will know that, when they give a neighbour an experience of genuine love, they are giving them an experience of God, because God is love. So our human love is a channelling of the love of God to one another. If this is not what happens when I love Mary Jane, then that love is not true. But if I channel God's love to others, then I will always love sensitively and well. Life is all about relationships.

Issuing from the fact that small Christian communities find their inspiration in the community of Father, Son and Holy Spirit, I found the people I consulted highlighted the following features:

- faith influencing life and leading to action,
- a strong prayerful dimension embracing the word of God, prayer, the eucharist, reflection and reconciliation,
- an emergence of 'the new person' referred to in Ephesians 4:24,
- sensitivity towards, and respect for, local cultures,
- the kingdom and its justice as the priority,
- a spirit of perseverance,
- a resistance towards the showy or flamboyant,
- a hunger for knowledge of God,
- a joyful spirit.

Laughter and the love of friends
Briefly, the spirituality of the small Christian communities might be graphically stated as befriending one another in God, Three in One. It's about intimacy. That love and relationships are of the essence has sometimes been expressed more vitally by secular rather than spiritual authors. Hilaire Belloc, for example, surely touches 'the burthen of the mystery' when he writes:

THREE DANCERS ONE DANCE

From quiet homes and first beginning,
Out to the undiscovered ends,
There's nothing worth the wear of winning,
But laughter and the love of friends.
(Dedicatory Ode)

* * *

My Niece Nearly Five

Cramped conditions favour her at four;
she twirls on a sixpence into dance
routines unrehearsed, broadcasts
original compositions through 15 yards
of green hose-pipe for silent millions.

Highly amused at her light foot sense
of fun, she delivers speeches to her
great grandchildren perched on the fence,
berating infants and mothers alike.

If you can be trusted, she will impart
one hundred thousand secrets only
she knows, giving everything away.
In the night sky she is the star beguiling
your exhausted world with fantasy.

The logic of your departure is beyond her,
but having squeezed the life out of you,
she whispers goodbye inside your jacket
where the lining smells of you.
(H.O'D)

5: Building Itself up in Love
(Way Forward for the Church)

It is most interesting to note how the disciples of Jesus gave practical expression to his message of love in the years following his death and resurrection. Small Christian communities sprang up in neighbourhoods – communities that were 'united, heart and soul' (Acts 4:32). So there were the house churches, yet there was also the preoccupation to come together in larger assemblies thus forming the communion of communities. So for a full experience of church, there seems to have been two concerns: firstly to be part of a small intimate community (cf Acts 12:12; Romans 16:5; Romans 16:11; Romans 16:14-15); then secondly there was the further concern to network with other communities thereby forming a communion of communities (cf Acts 2:46, 3:11, 14:26-27). The point that stands out, however, is that the early church was above all community or people of God. The emphasis was on persons.

Let us take two passages from the New Testament that show how community and full participation therein flourished in the early church.

Ephesians 4:14-16
We must no longer be children, tossed to and fro and blown about by every wind of doctrine, by people's trickery, by their craftiness in deceitful scheming. But speaking the truth in love, we must grow in every way into him who is the head, into Christ, from whom the whole body, joined and knit together by every ligament with which it is equipped, as each part is working properly, promotes the body's growth in building itself up in love.

This passage speaks eloquently of the union of Christians in Christ. We are parts of the body of which Christ is the head. In him we are knit together by every ligament; he promotes the body's growth in building itself up in love. The imagery expressing intimate union is powerful. Our business is to grow into the stature of Christ through living in unity. In the past priests were sometimes looked upon as the nexus, or neck, connecting the rest of the body to Christ the head. They mediated the relationship. Not so, we ordained priests are simply parts of the body of Christ, like all of his priestly people. There is only one mediator and that is Christ.

The church, then, is one in Christ; and the following passage clearly shows how fully the members shared in the workings of the community.

1 Corinthians 14:26-33
[26]What should be done, then, my friends? When you come together, each one has a hymn, a lesson, a revelation, a tongue or an interpretation. Let all things be done for building up. [27]If anyone speaks in a tongue, let there be only two or at most three, and each in turn; and let one interpret. [28]But if there is no one to interpret, let them be silent in church and speak to themselves and to God. [29]Let two or three prophets speak and let the others weigh what is said. [30]If a revelation is made to someone else sitting nearby, let the first be silent. [31]For you can all prophesy one by one, so that all may learn and all be encouraged. [32]And the spirits of the prophets are subject to the prophets, [33]for God is a God not of disorder but of peace.

Clearly there was full participation in early church liturgy, and liturgy is of the utmost importance to the Christian community. It follows, therefore, that there should be equal involvement in all other aspects of church life – including decision-making! It is also noteworthy that Paul ran into some of the problems that are commonly experienced in Christian celebrations even today: participants blurting out things together, some dominating, others rattling on and on while the listeners aren't sure of what they are talking about and no explanation is forthcoming. Such people also existed in the first century! He uses the epistle to suggest some points of order that will help communication – or prevent bedlam! The crucial issue, however, is that in the first-century church participation was complete. Also, the interventions described in the passage were routine; in verse 26 Paul uses the Greek word *(h)otan* for 'when' and *(h)otan* means 'whenever' rather than a once off 'when'.

* * *

A Jesus Prayer
(for Niamh and Ed)

Jesus you are
the lonesome cloud
    sailing celestial seas,
artist fashioning wide sky
    of radiant vermilion,
a distant star
    pulsing emerald, sapphire, gold,
the gleaming dove
    tumbling in gentle air,
o'erweening Everest,
Pacific phosphorescent.

Jesus you are
the hug
    of true friend,
the fair curl
on brow of drowsy child,
the prisoner
    in lonely cell
    waiting
    painfully,
the shaggy busker
    twanging his guitar
    to heedless crowds
    on city street,
pinch-faced mother
    with babe in flimsy shawl
    begging for loose change
    upon O'Connell Bridge,

> her fashion-plate sister too
> > gliding blithely by
> > unthinkingly.
>
> Jesus you are
> the hand that soothes
> > the fevered brow
> > of AIDS,
> soldier lowering rifle
> > to spare the life
> > of cowering foe
> > on poppied field.
>
> Jesus in a word
> your name is
> Love –
> love that smiles
> love that weeps
> love that never fails[19]
> (J.O'H)

---

19. James O'Halloran SDB, *In Search of Christ, A Prayer Book for Seekers*, Dublin: The Columba Press, 2004, pp 5-6.

6: Walking the Walk
(Commitment the Soul of Community)

One of the things that is said of the modern person is that they are reluctant to commit themselves. This is bad news for community, for if we want community, we have to be prepared to become wholeheartedly involved in the project. The same would hold for family. Unless there is this degree of dedication, there can be no question of it. Commitment is the soul of community. That Christian community, and more specifically the small Christian communities with which we have been dealing, presuppose faith in Jesus the Saviour goes without saying. There cannot be Christian commitment without belief in him because it calls for devotion to Christ and gospel values.

Being committed also presupposes conversion – that the members have taken seriously the responsibilities that come with baptism. At some point they have decisively turned their backs on what is evil and directed themselves towards the good. But then the consequences of that conversion have to be lived out, so that every day they struggle to become a little less selfish, a little more generous. Faith isn't simply a matter of ideas in the head, it translates into love-in-action. In other words, there is the continuous effort, as Paul puts it, to grow to the full stature of Christ (cf Ephesians 4:13). Paul intriguingly sees this happen through community as 'joined and knit together by every ligament' (Ephesians 4:16) we together build up the body of Christ. In doing so each one becomes more Christlike; hopefully one day they may be able to say with Paul '... it is no longer I who live, but it is Christ who lives in me' (Galatians 2:22).

When sharing on conversion and commitment with groups, I find it important to remind myself and those to whom I am speaking that this does not mean small communities are composed of angels. They are made up of sinners who in their brokenness often fall (cf Proverbs 24:16), yet steadfastly refuse to stay down. They always rise to seek reconciliation with God, neighbour and nature. Community is constantly being built up through continual reconciliation, and conversion needs constant affirmation. St John Bosco used to tell the young people for whom he worked that the tragedy lay not in falling, but in failing to rise again. And Dom Helder Camara writes: 'At the great judgement seat the Lord may say to someone: "How horrible! You fell a million times while on earth!" But all is salvaged if that person can say: "Yes, Lord, it really is frightful! But your grace helped me to get back on my feet a million and one times".'[20]

This leads to my own understanding of commitment as never ceasing to try, and I found instances of such commitment in my experience that would put one in mind of the Acts of the Apostles.

* * *

Mandla's Story
Following Mass in a remote African village one Sunday, Mandla approached Fr Victor a genial, dynamic, Italian priest.

'Fada, I would like to be baptised.'

The priest looked at the lad. He seemed really in earnest.

'Well now, if you want to be baptised, you must show me you mean business. First of all I want to see you here faithfully every Sunday and then, eventually, we can start preparing you for baptism.'

Every Sunday, without fail, Mandla was present at Mass. After quite some time he approached Fr Victor once more with his request.

The priest had noted his fidelity and now suggested that they consult with his parents.

'But my parents don't live in this village, Fada. Our home is in Makump.'

'Mama mia!' exclaimed Fr Victor in amazement. Makump was several hours away on foot along narrow paths between tall elephant grass. This boy was certainly determined.

---

20. Dom Helder Camara, *Hoping Against All Hope*, Maryknoll, New York, Orbis Books, 1964, p 189.

There was, however, a serious snag. Mandla's village was composed of Muslims and people who followed the native religion. The priest explained that were he to baptise him, he would be the sole Christian in the village. Without support, it would be most difficult for him to persevere in the faith. Under the circumstances the father felt that he could not baptise Mandla.

The lad was utterly crestfallen; tears stole down his cheeks. Father Victor was moved. Then he had an inspiration. 'I'll tell you what,' he said to the boy, 'if you are truly convinced that Jesus Christ is the Son of God, that he came on earth and died and rose to save us, that he wants us to love and help one another, then you will go back to your village and make him known to others. If you gather some people who, like yourself, freely desire baptism, we can give you the sacrament because you will have a support group.'

Two years after this encounter, I passed through Mandla's village with Fr Victor. The youth, by then a personable lad of fourteen, graciously offered me some fruit with both hands after the manner of Africa. In front of his house there was a large wooden cross painted in bold red. And Mandla had twenty adults and eighteen young people preparing for baptism with himself.

This achievement was all the more remarkable if we consider that young people are by no means the vocal element in African society that they are elsewhere. Perhaps the deciding factor was that Mandla not only spoke but acted as well, helping the old and the less able. In his actions, the word of God and prayer came alive. Jesus came alive.

(J.O'H)

The Old Man's Story
Equally moving is the story of an old man who lived in yet another African village. He was fast losing his sight owing to river blindness. In former times he had probably been searching the murky bottom of some river for diamonds and had become host to the parasite that causes this affliction. He went to a distant

hospital to stave off the darkness that was engulfing him. Apparently he left it too late. Although he was not cured, he did hear about Jesus Christ for the first time and the Lord touched him. In the loss of sight, he found new sight, rather like Gloucester in *King Lear*.

A Muslim himself, he went home to his Muslim brother and announced that he was a Christian. The brother, believing he was lost, banished him from the house. At his new lodging he beat the rim of an old car wheel every morning and evening to summon people. When he sensed there was a gathering, he would deliver his oft-repeated message: Jesus Christ, the Son of God, was born into this world and died and rose to save us. His great command was that we love one another. He could neither say The Lord's Prayer nor the Ave Maria.

Eventually Anthony, a travelling catechist, heard of the old man's work and went to speak with him. The veteran was overjoyed at meeting another Christian and had an insatiable desire to know more about Christ. He and the other people whom he had attracted to Jesus decided that they must have a little church.

The blind man worked generously at the building site. A child would lead him as he carried water or adobe blocks.

The effort, however, proved too much for him. One day he collapsed and was obviously dying. 'Get me the fada. I must be baptised,' he pleaded.

The priest was a six hour journey distant: three hours for the messenger to go, three hours for the father to come.

The old man lay gasping, refusing to die. After what seemed an age, the priest arrived and promptly baptised him. Ten minutes later he was dead – and with God forever.

(J.O'H)

The Peasant Missionaries
Twenty-five years ago, Bishop Leonidas Proaño, told me of a phenomenon that was happening in his diocese of Riobamba in Ecuador. Simple *campesinos* – peasants – moved by the Spirit

were going out from their own small Christian communities to encourage others to build similar ones. Usually, before the call, they had been dedicated members of their own groups with experience as co-ordinators.

When the call came, they donned poncho and hat as protection against the biting cold and bone-chilling mists of the Andes, slipped into their sandals and walked vast distances to bring the story of community to their brothers and sisters. They brought no social prestige with them, no material wealth and they were not ordained ministers: all they brought was the power of the word of God within them.

These missionaries created no structures, nor did they organise communities. What they did was to share experiences and enthuse local people to form their own groups.

While they were absent from their homes, their family and Indian neighbours looked after their tiny plots of land, livestock and meagre possessions. On coming back, their minds turned immediately to their next journey.

The bishop noted that the inspiration seemed to have come directly from the Holy Spirit, working among ordinary people. At the time there were forty such missionaries in the diocese of Riobamba – a consolation to its sorely tried bishop.

Curiously, on the other side of the world this same missionary story could be told of a Masai woman called Kati, who with her infant upon her back walked long distances to bring her fellow Masai the good news of Jesus Christ.

(J.O'H)

7: Theirs Not to Reason Why ...
(Effective Communication)

One of English comedian Tommy Cooper's quips was: 'Before I speak, I want to say a few words ...' Most people love to talk. Ah but listening is an entirely different proposition. Really listening. We have all been involved in conversations where the participants are not paying attention to one another, rather are they thinking of what they are going to say next or waiting impatiently to get in. Very likely we ourselves have been guilty of the same. Maybe we did not listen intently to others or observe the body language. There are different levels and even different ways of hearing: women, for example, hear differently from men. Unless we attend to all these factors, there will be no true 'listening' and, consequently, no communication. This is more injurious than we realise, because without communication there is no community. Communication is the oil that eases the wheels of community and, if we don't listen, without realising it, we get out of touch with life. We swirl about in our own cramped universe.

How do we deal with these obstacles to communication? The first thing is to become aware of them; no easy task if we have a blind spot in the matter. Perhaps we will read something and become aware of our deficiency, or maybe our failure to listen may land us in a crisis that forces us to think. Sometimes a person will say to us, 'You're just not listening!' Should this happen to me, I ought to examine myself carefully to see whether or not it is so.

I was co-ordinating a group at a parish gathering a short time ago. A lady made a suggestion regarding the creation of a prayer group. The type of group she was proposing wasn't down to earth and, though I acknowledged her suggestion, I didn't do so with much enthusiasm. The lady gave me a good verbal shake with a decisive: 'Now you listen to me!'

If I am an impulsive person, listening is difficult since it requires patience to sit silently and allow another to have their full say without interrupting. I have known people who have done this extremely well and I admired them greatly. I have to say they weren't too numerous. One man, in particular, I recall. It is Bishop Leonidas Proaño (RIP) of Ecuador, a great champion of human rights who was deservedly nominated for the Nobel Peace Prize. I certainly would have given him the Nobel Peace Prize and I would also have awarded him a Nobel Prize for Listening. He paid profound attention to what you said, did not hurry you, and when you had finished, waited for a time to ensure that you had said absolutely everything you wanted to. Only then would he respond and try to be helpful. You really got the sense of someone who was trying to stand in your shoes and walk with you. It's the process eloquently expressed by the Russian word – lovely to roll round in the mouth and a favourite of Mikhail Gorbachev – *perestroika*.

No communication no communion
And the relevance of communication to community? Without dialogue and consensus among the members of a community there can be no communion. Leaders of community who hand down decisions to the members without due consultation are engaged in a futile exercise. Decisions must be of the community and not just of individuals. Proposals can be made to the members, yet if they are not willing to accept them, they cannot be imposed. To do so would be useless; no real headway will be made, and eventually those pushing the process will find themselves back at square one. This would be a waste of time. Had they listened properly they would have discovered that people simply were not ready for what was asked. Knowing this the leaders might have been able to suggest a more constructive course, such as preparing the ground or raising consciousness. In our times, we have seen leaders take their nations to war against the wishes of their populations and the outcome has been catastrophic. And where is democracy in this? Ordinary people have a valid opinion too.

I was also at a meeting of a group once where a participant gave a member present a message from God, beginning with the awesome words, 'God wants you to ...' Poor God! The co-ordinator of the session thanked the person for the intervention but went on to add wisely that they would have to reflect on this matter in community. To seal such proposals there has to be prayer and discernment in community to see whether or not they are viable. We have of course to be sensitive to the possibility of a challenging prophetic utterance, while being wary of the solo run or the person who would manipulate God for their own purpose.

The days of 'theirs not to reason why' are fading. The millions who thronged the streets of cities throughout the planet to protest the Second Iraq War were a telling sign of the times. Dialogue, consultation and consensus constitute the pulse of the future, and the successful leaders and true democrats will be those who respect these realities. And thank heavens for that!

* * *

Trying to Boil a Kettle
When elected Auditor of a College Society
his first challenge was how to get a kettle boiled
for tea after evening meetings. The kitchen staff
said that they wouldn't be working overtime anymore.
He went to the Canteen Manageress who said the Union
would object to students boiling kettles for tea.
He went to the Warden who said he couldn't
interfere with the Manageress; anyway the students
would wreck anything they might lay their hands on.
He went to the Personnel Officer who said the Union
would hardly object, but what about fire insurance?
and besides he couldn't interfere with the Manageress.
He went to the Main Office and was advised to ask
the College Secretary for the required permission.
The Secretary listened for half and hour and said
he would note the point. *(Brian Power)*

Sound Advice for the White Rabbit
The White Rabbit put on his spectacles [to read a set of verses]. 'Where shall I begin, please your Majesty?' he asked.

'Begin at the beginning,' the King said, very gravely, 'and go on till you come to the end: then stop.'
(Lewis Carroll – from *Alice in Wonderland*)

8: That They May All Be One
(Unity Among Christians)

A church is Christian insofar as it is ecumenical, which means being open to the truth as it is experienced in various churches. There's nothing more urgent than being one in mind and heart. A most heartfelt prayer of Christ coming towards the end of his life was:

... that they may all be one;
As you, Father, are in me,
and I am in you ... (John 17:21).

So the question is never whether we will or will not do something about Christian unity. The only question is what exactly are we going to do? What is the best course of action in our situation?

But what is being done in actual fact? There have been symbolic gestures from our leaders. Pope Paul VI's embrace of the Greek Orthodox Patriarch Athenagoras and of the Archbishop of Canterbury were such. So too was Pope John Paul's famous meeting with religious leaders of the world in Assisi. More recently we have had the visits of Pope Benedict XVI to a mosque and a synagogue.These gestures were significant, yet do not seem to me to have had the follow-up that they promised. It is encouraging to hear Benedict XVI's call for real progress on unity.

Two fronts
I think there has to be a two-pronged approach to the issue, theological and practical. There has been progress at the level of theology. For example, the recent document from ARCIC (Anglo-Roman Catholic International Commission) *Mary, Grace and Hope in Christ* is truly significant and could prove a historic breakthrough. It declares that, properly understood, Anglicans can accept the Marian content of the two dogmas of the Immaculate Conception and Asumption. The faith-and-works controversy between Lutherans and Catholics has also been re-

solved. Controversy over the eucharist, papal primacy, the ordination of women priests and an openly gay bishop, however, has considerably slowed down progress between Rome and Canterbury. Regarding such theological progress that has been made, we still have to reap the full practical benefits.

There have been actual advances at the grassroots and these, perhaps, have been the most encouraging aspect of the ecumenical movement so far. I myself am a member of a small Christian community in Dublin, which, though composed entirely of Catholics, is nevertheless very ecumenically minded. We have tried to link up with the local Church of Ireland (Anglican) community, attended the meetings of interdenominational groups, invited people of other denominations, even other religions to come and chat and pray with us. We have been in demonstrations of various kinds with members of different denominations and indeed of none. Olive, an ordained priest of the Church of Ireland, spent a year as a member of our community. Her cheerful presence enriched us enormously. The group, though mature, is youthful on the whole and seems to have no trouble in being marvelously open. Efforts such as these would not be unique to our group, rather would they be reasonably common nowadays. Small communities are powerful instruments for bringing about unity.

I have just mentioned how people of disparate denominations, for example, joined to demonstrate for worthy causes. There are practical things we can do well together. To sink a well, build a bridge or struggle to have prisoners-of-conscience released are matters on which we can all co-operate. After all, there is no such thing as a Catholic, Protestant or Muslim bridge: bridges are ecumenical and allow everyone, whatever their race or creed, to cross a river in safety.

Personal testimony
In my work to promote small Christian communities I have shared with all denominations and I found less and less difficulties in this. Why shouldn't I feel at ease with fellow Christians;

we are family. As I said to a Church of Ireland group I was working with recently, 'We have one over-riding thing in common. We have the same boss.' I heard a distinct sigh of approbation in the room. If I say, 'Some of my best friends are Protestant,' I know it may sound like a cliché. But it is true. Not only have they been great friends to me, they have also been wonderful spiritual friends and guides. When I work with them I am true to my Catholic identity, just as they are true to their particular identity. I am so happy if our sharing leads them to be better Anglicans, Baptists or whatever, as it can lead me to try and be a better Catholic.

Dietrich Bonhoeffer did not subscribe to easy grace, nor do I subscribe to easy ecumenism. We Christians have been divided for centuries and time is needed to sort out differences and heal wounds. We shouldn't put pressure on the consciences of people to do something with which they don't feel comfortable, though they might dearly wish to. We participate to the degree that we are able. All of us have constraints depending on the times in which we live, even Jesus had such constraints. One such was that he was sent to minister to the lost sheep of the house of Israel (Matthew 15:24) and was put in a quandary when gentiles sought his intervention. Yet the interesting thing is that he always responded to faith and dialogue; we saw him do so with the Canaanite woman (Matthew 15:21-28) and the Roman centurion (8:5-13).

Although we have to struggle against constraints, in the more than thirty years that I have been working with small Christian communities, I have been frequently challenged by the Spirit to openness. I can fully sympathise with the dilemma of Peter in the household of the gentile Cornelius as he asks, 'Could anyone refuse the waters of baptism to the people, now they have received the Holy Spirit as much as we have' (Acts 10:47). Again Peter, like Jesus, was responding to the faith that was so evident in that household. Indeed all of Acts chapter 10 makes for absorbing reading in the light of ecumenism.

In conclusion, my hope and prayer is that church leaders and scholars will match the endeavour of God's people in the effort to respond to Christ's ardent prayer, 'That they may all be one.' If this is done, then progress will be at the pace God intends. And, as you often see written by Muslims on trucks in West Africa: 'God time is best!' And speaking of Africa, I believe that it has much of value to say to us on the subject of ecumenism, as will be seen in our next chapter.

* * *

Eucharist and Community
The word eucharist means 'thanksgiving'. Above all it is thanksgiving for, and a celebration of, unity – of the efforts we make in families and small communities to be one. When the presiding minister raises the host, we are powerfully challenged to be body of Christ. It is as if Christ were saying, 'I am communion. Now you go out and be communion too.' 'Though we are many, we all become one, for we share in the one bread and the one cup' (1 Corinthians 10:16-17). How can we possibly partake of these mysteries and fail to be united? If people riven by class division celebrate the sacrament, it becomes an empty gesture. With the Christians in Corinth who are falling into this error, Paul is blunt: 'It is not the Lord's supper you are celebrating' (1 Corinthians 11:20).[21]

---

21. James O'Halloran SDB, *Small Christian Communities, Vision and Practicalities*, Dublin: The Columba Press, 2002, pp 49-50.

9: Dragging No Elephant
(Ecumenism in Africa)

Regarding ecumenism, I have found Africa of great interest. Over most of that vast continent – there are some sad exceptions – it doesn't present the difficulties that it does elsewhere in the world, because even within extended families you have members of varying denominations. I heard a bishop tell of how in his extended family there were Roman Catholics, Seventh Day Adventists and people who professed the native African religion. It really depended on the school they had attended as children. Yet they all lived together in harmony; as the bishop so rightly said, 'We can't afford to do otherwise.' Where ecumenism is concerned, we in Europe are hampered by the baggage of history. Africans, however, see no reason why they should have to drag that particular elephant through the desert. How sad it would be if Christianity were to bring rifts into families that were traditionally united. It would be the antithesis of what it is about.

An African cardinal once told Pope John Paul II that his father was a chief who professed the native religion and had eight wives. 'And you are now a cardinal!' marvelled the pope. Indeed the cardinal's progression was even more amazing than that of the nineteenth century Archbishop Ullathorne of Birmingham, England, whose autobiography was entitled, *From Cabin Boy to Archbishop*. Not surprisingly there were those who balked at the buccaneering flavour of this title and suggested sanitising it to the more appropriate *From Altar Boy to Archbishop*. The feisty Ullathorne would have none of it.

Unity in diversity
Indeed depending on where you lived in Africa, you could have family members belonging to, not simply other Christian denominations, but different religions as well. Relating to fellow Christians, therefore, is hardly an issue at all. I have a friend,

Joachim, who is going to be a Catholic priest whereas his sister is studying to be a Pentecostal pastor. They both deeply love and respect each other and their mother said, 'I am happy because you are both doing something good.' Are Africans not saying to us that the eventual unity of all Christians will be a unity in diversity?

This is my own belief. Many denominations have quite a tradition built up now. Rather than expecting people to become part of some great Christian melting pot, could we not look at the possibility of different rites within a unified whole? The differences could enrich and strengthen our unity.

Even members of different religions, Christian and Muslim for example, relate easily in the African context and can work together. Again they can be from the same extended family so how could it sensibly be otherwise? Fr Tony in Sierra Leone was celebrating the eucharist in a small village on the occasion of the harvest festival. The church was packed largely with Muslims. Before the ceremony was finished, the muezzin in the tower of the nearby mosque started calling all his co-religionists to prayer, because it was Friday. Nobody stirred in the church: all reverently remained until the Mass concluded. Then the Muslims trooped off faithfully to the mosque. I have been at Christian funerals where the great majority of those praying for the soul of the departed have been Muslims; the Christians would have the same openness. Here surely is a sign of great hope for churches, religions and the world.

* * *

Ecumenical Pilgrimage 1996

It was at the end of our journeying
through desert and city in the Holy Land
that we took the road to Emmaus.
We travelled by coach – not walking
as Clopas and his close companion
perhaps his wife seem to have done.
We were moving too fast for Christ
until we met him in a Crusader's church
hewn from rock surrounded by bougainvillea
in the breaking of the bread and blending of
our voices in glory to the risen Lord.
Then all was done. We went our separate ways
to churches and communities different
but newly bonded in a common hope.
Thine be the glory risen conquering Lord
dissolving our suspicion and our fear.
A warm and healing journey did we not have of it?
(Brian Power)

10: Building Bridges: Building Kingdom
(Forging a Better World)

When we talk about the church, we are talking family really. What of the great world beyond this family? There we find people of all creeds and none at all. The most important thing for Jesus in his ministry was what he would call the kingdom of God and its justice (cf Matthew 6:33). The word 'church' is used only three times in the gospels (cf Matthew 16:18; 18:17) while Christ speaks frequently of the kingdom. It is 'the absolute good' to which everything else must defer.[22] And if the kingdom is the priority for the founder of Christianity, surely it must also be the priority for his followers too? But in what does it consist?

There is no defining the kingdom because we are into the area of mystery. We could volunteer the following in an attempt to describe it:

- 'a new creation' (Galatians 6:15; Revelations 21:1).
- the priority (Matthew 6:33; Luke 12:31).
- God's rule prevailing in the world (Psalm 103:19).
- the person of Jesus: his mind, heart and values (cf. Matthew 16:28; 19:29; Mark 9:1; Luke 9:27; seen widely in the 'I am' statements in John's gospel).
- wherever there is harmony rooted in justice (Matthew 6:33; Luke 12:31).
- all that is good, gracious and therefore, God-revealing – where 'the blind see, the lame walk' (Luke 7:21), and where 'I was hungry and you fed me, thirsty and you gave me a drink' (Matthew 25:35).
- openness and tolerance (Matthew 20:1-16; Acts 5:34-39).
- present and yet to come (1 Corinthians 15:12-28).

Harmony would be the sustained note of God's kingdom, though in it we find some strange bedfellows indeed, as the beautiful images of the prophet strikingly illustrate:

---

22. Paul VI, *The Evangelisation of Peoples*, Dublin: Dominican Publications, 1977, no 8.

> The wolf shall live with the lamb
> the leopard shall lie down with the kid,
> the calf and the lion and the fatling together,
> and a little child shall lead them (Isaiah 11:6).

Note the emphasis on harmony, again there is the implication of community. The kingdom is a matter of cohesion rooted in justice. It is wherever there is genuine goodness, and it matters not whether the goodness is found among Muslims, Hindus, Buddhists, Jews or people who would profess no religion – we will support it, as a priority. As already noted, there are no purely Catholic bridges. This opens up a world vista for us beyond our particular persuasion. Our first concern must be to work for a better world and we are not simply talking about the hereafter, but also of the here and now: 'a new heaven and a new earth' (Revelations 21:1).

We say that the kingdom is wherever we find goodness. This story would be an example. A valued friend of mine died during the year (2004). Towards the end he spent quite a time in hospital and during all that period his wife rarely left his side. I was amazed at her endurance. No wonder the man, who wrote poetry, penned a work in her honour (it follows this piece).

I'd like to give a further example, this time from Latin America. I came across an elderly woman who, although in her seventies, was doing back-breaking work building roads. On enquiring, I found out that she was doing this to support her daughter who was lying at home in bed dying painfully of cancer. Moved by the old woman's plight, I contacted friends in Ireland and got some money. Because of the fantastic exchange rate, it amounted to a considerable sum, so that she was able to leave the work and stay at home to look after her daughter as she wished to do. She was also able to afford soothing medication. The great love of that mother was truly a sign of the kingdom. Besides, the episode made me think. There were thousands of people in equally dire situations and, while I could help some, helping all was impossible. I began to ask myself if there was any way of getting to the root of these problems. It was then that I became aware of how people, though poor, shared as best they could and I realised small communities that would network with one another could be powerful instruments for justice.

Christ must increase
As a Christian, I am not seeking to diminish Christ or his message, when I say that the kingdom is found beyond the confines of the Christian churches. I believe that he is the key to our whole human destiny, and I would be delighted if the whole world were to become his disciples. Nor am I trying to diminish his church; I love my church. As a young person I mistakenly equated it with the kingdom but I now know that this is not so. The church is of course part of the kingdom, should give powerful witness to it and be an effective instrument for implementing it in society. But it is not the totality of the kingdom.

I have to say that I find the whole vision of the kingdom liberating. It throws open windows and shutters and allows fresh air, light and sunshine to come flooding in. Above all, the reality of the kingdom helped me to flesh out my own vision for the church and the world, as given above. Let me recall it for the reader (it is in fact both vision and strategy): I encourage small Christian communities and would have them link with one another in larger entities, so as to form a communion of communities. I would, however, promote groups of all kinds, whether religious or civil (secular), that are doing anything to build a better world and would have them network with and support one another in the doing of good. Having seen the potential of such positive groupings when they link up, I am convinced that such a force at the grassroots would not merely reform society, it would renew it.

* * *

Dolores Sign of the Kingdom

I saw you standing on your own,
your beauty unsurpassed,
and though the years have slipped away
your loveliness still lasts.
For beauty was not all I saw
that first eventful day,
but a warm and tender playful girl
that swept my heart away.

Although the years are fading fast
and our lives are on the wane,
that first and precious love we shared
will always be the same.
For youth and beauty cannot last,
we grow old for all to see,
and though we're in our twilight years,
you're still beautiful to me.
(Liam Nolan)

11: Christopher, I Owe You
(Having a Sense of Process)

The staples of community for me would be:
- bonding,
- spirituality,
- reality/action,
- commitment,
- communication.

As you can well imagine, you cannot wave a wand and produce these characteristics instantly. There is a lengthy process involved that must take account of natural rhythms. So in this age of instant tea, instant coffee, microwave ovens and swiftly responding broad band computers, we have to develop a sense of process, which is by no means easy. We have lost the habit. There has to be the realisation that anything significant cannot be built in a day, least of all relationships. Patience and the ability to delay satisfaction are vital life skills.

People today are often disappointed when their efforts are not rewarded with immediate results. I recall an occasion in Ghana when, as usual, I had been sharing with a group on the subject of small Christian communities. The discussion was difficult. Lots of roadblocks. When it was all over, I must have looked somewhat bedraggled, even dispirited, because a man called Christopher approached and told me the following story:

> Fr James, I am an agricultural instructor and my work is to help the farmers in the locality. Twenty years ago, hoes were the only tools used for cultivation around here. In the cause of progress we decided to get the farmers using oxen instead for ploughing, so we decided to provide a team of oxen for every one of them. And you know what happened? They ate the oxen! But now, twenty years later, I can tell you, Fr James, that oxen are used for ploughing all over this area. And twenty years from now, there will be small Christian communities all over this area.

It is now twenty years later, and Christopher was right.

Obviously what he was telling me was that, though his solution to the sole use of hoes was actually eaten, he did not throw his hands up in despair, but set about slowly changing the minds and customs of people. In other words he grasped that there was a process involved. Something that had gone on for centuries could not be changed overnight; from hoe to plough was a considerable technological leap. No doubt there were many more lapses and disappointments along the road before the new method was fully accepted. Even a few more juicy sirloin steaks may have been thoughtlessly consumed.

Many things happened to me and many things were said during long years of travel and work. Only some of them have stayed in my mind. Perhaps they were the events and words that most deeply impressed me. I have never forgotten the prophetic Christopher, a slight man with narrow face, greying hair and dark intelligent eyes. He brought home to me the utter importance of having a sense of process and gave my spirits such a lift that I can feel the exhilaration to this day.

Thanks Christopher; I owe you.

* * *

Guru of the Sixties

Back and forth you shuttled
a whirlwind crossing
the Irish Channel
to sit crosslegged on threadbare
carpets in student bedsitters
feeding open-mouthed fledgings
constructing a new God.
My mind schemed how
to join this revolution
without – yes without
being noticed by those
with power to burn me.
Recreating God can be
a dangerous business. *(Brian Power)*

PART THREE

Education

1: Small But Worthwhile
(Education for Freedom)

The most startling information about formal education is the vast number of people who get none. According to the UN Human Development Report 2003, there are 680 million children of primary school age in developing countries. Of these a staggering 115 million do not attend school – significantly three fifths of them are girls. In India 40 million children are not in primary school, more than a third of the world's total. Furthermore, the fact that someone begins primary school doesn't at all mean that they will finish because half of those who start never finish. In Sub-Saharan Africa only one in three makes it all the way through primary. Small wonder then that a quarter of the adults in the developing world cannot read or write. So to survive until secondary school you have to be extremely fortunate, while getting to university would be the equivalent of winning the lottery.

Not that the developed world doesn't have its problems where education is concerned. There are run-down areas where disciplinary problems are enormous and motivation is lacking because of an impoverished social background. Unemployment is endemic in such areas and to make matters worse the parents are not given a fair slice of the economic cake. These circumstances engender indifference, absenteeism and premature abandonment of the whole educational project – even by promising students.

What to do about all this? There aren't easy answers. Obviously, the educational deprivation in the developing countries has to be seen as part of the wider picture of poverty. As already mentioned elsewhere, if the political will was there, this is something that can be solved. The same would be true of the difficulties experienced in the developed world. It's not enough to offer free education in a deprived area, resources have to be devoted also to addressing the wider social malaise.

Baffling poetry

Of modern poetry someone has said: 'Most people don't like poetry, because most poetry doesn't like people.' About education we could say something similar: Many students don't like education, because education doesn't like many students. It is a question of providing functionaries for the prevailing capitalist economy and is, therefore, dominated by pragmatism. There is more room for the subjects that serve this objective than those that do not. Computer science, for example, would be held in greater esteem than the classics, which have fallen on hard times. There is still too much of pupils sitting in serried rows passively absorbing information in preparation for stressful examinations that can summarily decide their future careers. So education is more industry-centred than person-centred. This distorts what it is all about. The question we have to face is whether we think education is liberating people and helping them to think for themselves or is it inducting them into the prevailing ideology. Surely it means that we form thoughtful and compassionate human beings and not just produce automatons for industry and commerce. Which is not saying that we don't need persons qualified in these fields. But it should not be to the detriment of imagination and creativity.

Even within the prevailing system, good teachers can do much to impart values and foster creativity and imagination. Indeed they already do so, despite the constraints. I tried to do it myself. Many of the stratagems I will describe in chapter 3 of this section, I employed in regular school classrooms, though what I will be describing in 3 is an alternative approach. One must pay tribute also to community schools that strive successfully to bring pupils, teachers and parents together to form a united force for the benefit of their common educational project. The concern to form pupils so that they will take their place in society as good human beings and upright citizens is admirable. Truth to tell, we are all caught in systems. Systems are never radical because we have to settle for the average opinion of the masses. Yet don't despair, seek out and work with like-minded people (groups/communities) for a better world. And make sure that you are not dehumanised by systems. Even within totalitarian political situations, down there in the engine-room of the operation, striving to put bread on the table for their families, I found sterling people who would quietly help you in a crisis.

Needless to say, the young people who would benefit most of all from a liberating, proactive approach to education are the ones with whom we are most concerned in this piece. I speak of those who are getting no education at all, not even primary. I speak also of the wilder ones who can't fit into our current patterns. Alternative forms of pedagogy are called for. I recall having one of the supposedly less able classes, numbering about forty-five lads – how did I survive? – in a Liverpool comprehensive school. I was teaching them English and was expending three-quarters of my energy on discipline and one quarter on teaching. Then I had an idea. I got them all a copybook and asked them to write *My Life* on the cover and set about giving a full account of their existence up to that point. I have to say that this was one of my successes. You could hear a pin drop as they beavered away. And one boy in particular whom I used to feel like 'malafoostering', to use my mother's menacing expression, would call me eagerly to come and see what he had written. Another boy had the nickname 'God' because he knew everything! His work was entitled *God - an Autobiography*. I'm sure he went far in life.

In conclusion I would like to return to where I began and deplore the fact that so many of the least of our brothers and sisters go without a formal education. I would wish for a liberating education for them. Indeed I would be delighted if all young people could have one. There must be something, even a small thing that we can do for those who never learn to read or write. Experience has shown me it won't go unrewarded.

* * *

A Small Good Thing
I was trying to teach a young lad from the travelling community in Ireland to read and write some years ago. It was one of the most frustrating teaching assignments I'd ever had. Every time he turned up for a lesson he had totally forgotten what we had done in the previous one. So we went on repeating and repeating Lesson 1, until it became like a needle stuck on an old 78 record. Then one day he came in a bit excited. 'I was out in the Hiace with me brudder yesterday,' he told me, 'and I saw dis word on de road sayin' S-T-O-P. I knew wha' it meant an' I shouted at me brudder STOP an' he braked. Looky, 'cos dey was a big 'ticulated lorry comin' dat would have kilt us stone dead, so it would!' This gave a new urgency to Lesson 1, and I returned to it with zest.

(J.O'H)

2: Free to Soar
(A Liberating Education)

An explanation for part of the difficulties around education has to do with the manner of it. In the previous essay I said that education should be liberating and, in my experience, very often it is not. It should set the spirit of the pupil free to soar, not keep it 'cabined, cribbed, confined'. A liberating education would be strong on participation. It would try to draw out from the student what is within, help them to articulate it. This approach is two way: sometimes the teacher becomes the pupil and the pupil the teacher. Primarily education ought to be about getting people to think for themselves; it is not about pouring information into passive, unquestioning recipients. The teacher is the 'midwife' who facilitates the process that encourages them to think and express themselves. I'm not saying that there should not be input by the teacher. Sometimes to get an abundant flow of water from a pump, you have to put a little into it. It's called priming the pump. The same has to be done with students. No, not pour some water down their throats, but impart some stimulating information that will hopefully call forth a flood of ideas.

I was fortunate to have a wise tutor as I trained to be a teacher. Why not honour him? His name was Harold Loukes and he was a professor in the Education Department at Oxford. As part of our training we spent a term doing teaching practice in a school. Foolishly brave, I opted for a huge comprehensive school in a working people's area of Liverpool – it was a great experience. Actually it was the school I mentioned in the previous chapter. While I was there, Mr Loukes came to supervise my teaching. He sat in on an English class I gave. Afterwards he offered me one of the best pieces of advice I ever got. 'James,' he said, 'when you are giving input, the pupils may be learning, maybe not. But when you set them to work, you know they are learning.' Reading between the lines, he was saying keep input to the minimum (young people can dream during input) and work the students to the maximum individually or, better still, in groups. The pedagogue who thought up and fostered a liberating education (*educación liberadora*) was the Brazilian Paulo Freire. For me, however, Harold Loukes was a simple, though not simplistic, Paulo Freire before I ever even heard of the latter.

Both these men had another concern in their teaching. Above all, they wanted to communicate values. Freire's impact on intellectual and indeed political life in Latin America was considerable. He taught in a manner that raised the awareness of people and awakened thousands to the oppression they were enduring. For example, when teaching downtrodden peasants to read, there would be a chart with a picture of a peasant's wretched hut and on the same chart a luxurious dwelling. Under each would be written the word 'house'. Obviously there were houses and houses. Decoding the chart could take you far afield; it could eventually bring you to the heart of the prevailing social problem. Having been exposed to Freire's method for a relatively short time, a poor Indian had a blinding insight: 'The landowners say we Indians are drunkards, we are not drunkards, we are oppressed.' Freire's method had made him think, so that he got to the root cause of the drinking problem. This procedure has the unwieldy name 'conscientisation'. It consists of growing in awareness, through continual and progressive action and reflection with a view to going out and modifying the world. It's not a matter simply of being more aware for the satisfaction of being aware, but to use the enhanced awareness to build a better society.

In Latin America I found a school that totally embraced the *educación liberadora* (liberating education) of Paulo Freire and you'd have to say that the students were most appreciative of the method. The manner in which they thought for themselves and reached out to the needy was impressive. However, not everyone was comfortable with young people who thought for themselves. Surprise, surprise!

* * *

Autumn Conference
The golds of autumn scattered morning mists
as one by one we trailed to the conference hall
where the Whiz Kid greeted us. It cost
a thousand pounds to have the Kid delivered
to teach us how to manage a wilting church
(some of us could barely manage getting out of bed).
Oh he was human, charming, exuding wit,
a young man who adored his wife and child.
So his asides revealed as he consumed
two flip-charts with his PERSONAL REFLECTIVENESS
models and FORWARD PLANNING techniques.
I could love you, Whiz Kid, if you'd only stop
and tell us more about your wife and child.
(Brian Power)

3: No Compulsion
(Imaginative Educational Alternatives)

I strongly believe that we need alternative systems of education. Some youngsters are total misfits in a system that expects them to sit more or less passively in desks and absorb information. The whole social background from which they come may militate against it. So the issue of social deprivation has to be addressed if progress is to be made at the level of school. Lateral thinking regarding hands-on, imaginative alternatives to our present methods have to be explored. I have spent many years of my life working within the formal educational scene. However, for over thirty I have also had the good fortune to be involved in a participative, liberating educational project on all continents.

The subject mostly under consideration for this project is: 'The Vision and Practicalities of Small Christian Communities.' The vision entails consideration of the theology and spirituality of community, while the practicalities deal with items such as starting groups, organisation, leadership, meetings, outreach and the like.

Voluntary Students

Significantly, participants come to these courses or workshops of their own free choice. The sessions are advertised and people encouraged to come but ultimately it has to be their own decision. They come because they are personally interested in what is on offer and feel it will enrich their lives. There are no examinations with their consequent diplomas at the end, so there isn't this stress attached to the exercise. It can't be a matter of the course being secondary to getting the diploma. This, I find, makes a notable difference to the atmosphere in which work is done and enhances the educational process. In short, the participants are enthusiastic about learning as much as they can because they feel it will enhance their lives. I'm sure there are important lessons to be learned about education from this.

Typical of these groups would be one I had in Ikelenge, Zambia, in the eighties. They were farmers who voluntarily left their holdings for a week to share on the subject of community. Could you imagine this happening in the industrialised world where we all labour under the tyranny of time? One day a goat that had been dispatched arrived on the scene. There was great rejoicing as everyone looked forward to a barbecue. Then it was discovered that the animal had been killed by lightning, and it was taboo to eat anything that had been killed by lightning which came from the heavens. It would be unlucky. A liberating education was called for.

A Community Spirit
I find that the most telling factor of all in our sessions is that a community spirit prevails. The participants come in groups, so some of them know each other well even before the course or workshop begins. Then there is the advantage that Africans are by nature, and indeed practice, communitarian anyway. I am convinced that true education only happens in a context of community. It is something that, from my point of view, I would like to emphasise.

Method used
Through the years I refined the method. Usually I had been invited by people on the spot to give the workshops, so I began to operate with local teams in doing the work. This meant that a team with some experience remained to continue the work once I departed. The courses, in fact, took the form of a symposium in which all took an active part, so no one was left without some expertise. The process was participative: all were teachers and all were pupils. I would begin by asking those taking part a question like, 'Have you had experience of being a member of a group of any kind and what did you find helpful in the exercise and what were the difficulties?' People would then work for a time in buzz groups of three or four that would form naturally. Once this was finished, the participants would share in a sponta-

neous, non-formal way regarding features they found helpful and those that were not so.

I always find this session quite helpful, because it gives you a feel for the people present and can give direction for the workshop. You have to listen with the utmost care and respect to what people are saying and not answer questions that have not been asked in the first place. As mentioned, in this process the teacher often exchanges role with the pupil.

Taking into account what transpired in the buzz groups, I then proceed to share my own thoughts on the subject under consideration with the group. This with a view to motivating their own thinking rather than trying to fill them with information.

Group work would be next on the agenda. A solid session to give the participants a chance to reflect on what had sparked them in the session thus far. Rather than tedious reports, the groups would be encouraged to share in a spontaneous way on the more striking items and insights. It is, I believe, in forums like these that the real learning takes place.

A course can be spread over some days and optimum times chosen. In a workshop, however, you work intensively for a couple of days and, despite a good break for lunch, have to use the afternoons – which can be drowsy! Something that keeps the participants active is called for. A pilot community meeting for the group(s) is a strategy I often use. Here all can join, for example, in a Bible sharing that filters what has been said regarding community through the word of God. This hammers home the lessons learned. Nights are for entertainment. But the social coming together is as important as coming together to acquire knowledge, especially if the subject is community. Worship is, of course, an integral part of the programme.

And so it goes. The foregoing gives an idea of the basic dynamic of this educational approach. All sorts of stratagems are used to add spice to proceedings: open forums as clearing houses for ideas and questions, group work of varying kinds, brainstormings, communing with nature, group dynamics, audiovisuals, drama, music and song, dance and so forth. The main features of the method are that it has to be liberating and participative. In courses very often, the input is at the theoretic and inspirational level but, when the course is over, the participants don't quite know what to do about it. Talk about the group skills involved, such as the ability to dialogue, share on the scriptures and pray is not enough. We need to 'do' them. The participants then have the practical tools with which to continue. And before the participants depart the scene, they are asked to share regarding what practically they are going to do as a result of the workshop.

Finally, I must say that I find sessions such as these more life-giving for myself than work in formal educational settings. The same, I believe, would be true of the participants.

* * *

De-schooling
Attention!
Today we will finish creation.
(H.O'D)

Schooling
The hours in school-grey, shadows
bullied out of poor light, corridors
meeting in a dead end; it is night,
it seems, for six months of the year.

All that happens here is subject
to eternity, down to a teardrop spreading
on a page; God must not find us
out of our beds, or picking a path
through the woods to a lake ...

My child, you have broken silence,
swapped towels with older boys,
been caught barefoot out of bounds –
I tell you it will not go as hard with Sodom
as with you on Judgement Day. *(H.O'D)*

4: John Bosco Educator
(A Fool for Christ)

Who was John Bosco? You may well ask. He was an Italian priest born near Turin, Italy, in 1815. He was usually known as Don Bosco, 'Don' being the familiar name for Father. Different he was. So different that two prelates tried on one occasion to commit him to what was then called a lunatic asylum: nowadays, more benignly, a psychiatric facility. They arranged for a pleasant outing in the country. The plan was to have Don Bosco enter the carriage first, then slam the door on him and have the driver of the carriage head helter-skelter for the asylum. The trouble was that Don Bosco guessed at what was afoot and deferentially urged the two reverends to enter the carriage first. They had no option then, they felt, but to accompany him. But as soon as they had entered, it was Don Bosco who slammed the door and the carriage raced to its destination. The people at the asylum were surprised to find two deranged priests instead of the one expected and the lofty prelates had a devil of a time trying to convince the authorities of their sanity. The more loudly they protested the more suspicious the authorities grew. But never again did anyone doubt John Bosco's sanity!

Their reason for thinking Don Bosco unhinged in the first place was revealing. As a boy of nine he had a dream in which Jesus and Mary urged that he devote himself to young people. He never forgot this dream and soon after his ordination in 1841 started working with poor and abandoned boys. Because of this work, he was destined to be remembered forever as the Friend of Youth. The number of these urchins was to increase dramatically as they were thrown on to the streets of big cities like Turin by the Industrial Revolution and the wars of 1848. Indeed after those wars there were many homeless orphans. In effect those young people were internal refugees. It was in Turin that Bosco launched his work.

But to get back to the asylum incident. Priests in Italy at that time felt that a certain aloofness was appropriate. As a boy John Bosco lamented this and was determined that, if he became a priest, he would be different. And as we said above, being different landed him in trouble. On Sundays he marched his ragamuffins through the streets looking for a place to play; he was also searching for a home for those boys. Dash it! He even flew about in his soutane playing football with them. A priest simply didn't do these things. It was not regarded as appropriate behaviour – which was why they tried to put him away.

Don Bosco's work was blessed and it thrived. Eventually he founded the Salesian Congregation ('Salesian' for its patron the gentle St Francis de Sales) to carry on his project for young people all over the world. With Mary of Mornese he also founded the Daughters of Mary Help of Christians to do for girls what he was doing for boys. Mixed schools weren't the rage back in those days! The Daughters also grew apace and have now spread to all continents. Worn out by his endeavours, Don Bosco died in 1888 and on Easter Sunday, 1934, was declared a saint by Pope Pius XI. Aptly, for one who made himself a fool for Christ, it was April Fools' Day. Well, he nearly did get himself locked up in a lunatic asylum.

The foregoing completes the biographical sketch. We now need to take a closer look at the practical aspects of Don Bosco's approach to education.

* * *

My Story

It is a quantum leap from Turin in the eighteen hundreds to the Salesian College, Pallaskenry, County Limerick, Ireland, in 1947. On 13 September that year, I entered the college. Corporal punishment was common in schools in those days and I had been to such schools. I was one of those pupils who could not be motivated by corporal punishment. There was no such punishment in Pallaskenry. Don Bosco had ruled it out in his schools and youth centres a hundred years before and this school was true to Don Bosco's way. I was so relieved. My first letter home spoke in glowing terms of this. But there was much more to Pallaskenry. Our Salesian teachers were really friendly with us. A family, or Salesian, spirit prevailed in the place.

As part of the staff you had the brothers: these were seminarists who interrupted their studies to do three practical years at the school before returning to complete those studies in what was known as the theologate – nothing to do with Watergate. The brothers weren't much older than some of the students they were teaching and were almost 'buddies' to them. They gave the place a feeling of youth and vitality, accompanied us in study and play. The interesting thing was that you would be quite familiar with them in the playground but this in no way impaired your respect for them in the classroom. But perhaps the thing that most impressed me was how well the Salesian community got on together and the good-humour that prevailed among them. I felt I would like to be part of all this, so I went on to become a Salesian myself.

(J.O'H)

5: The Salesian Way
(Don Bosco's Preventive System)

On becoming a Salesian, I learned more about the educational approach from which I had benefited as a lad and realised that Don Bosco had something unique to share with the world. The most important feature was his concern to provide education for 'the poor and the abandoned', those who without him would receive none. This was the major concern of his life. As we have already seen, where education is concerned, there is no greater problem in today's world than that of those who miss out totally on it.

To head off problems even before they commenced was his strategy. For example, take the modern issue of drugs: getting a young person off drugs is infinitely harder than preventing them from starting in the first place.

How did Don Bosco help young people from taking wrong paths? His method had strong spiritual elements. Maybe it would be better to speak of a spirituality of education rather than a method, which suggests mere classroom practice. Regarding classroom practice, he was quite eclectic, a magpie who would pick up on any helpful procedure from wherever it came.

He prevented those deprived young people for whom he worked from getting into trouble by keeping them occupied and filling their minds and hearts with all that is good and wholesome. For him and his followers today, keeping young people occupied would not be simply a matter of sitting them down in front of a computer or video. He was an advocate of healthy outdoor activities, as we have seen (he even got permission to take young offenders out of jail for hikes). His mother, Mamma Margaret, gave him a great appreciation of nature; she would take him out at night to admire the glory of the stars. Imagine what they looked like in those days before light pollution. He was creative in thinking up ways of keeping his boys busy:

THE SALESIAN WAY

drama, choral music, brass band, orchestra, art and so forth were all employed. And not least, he would have them take their technical training and studies seriously. Friendly presence, or availability, was a vital part of his way. John Bosco was unobtrusively present among his boys, accompanying them in their activities, just as the good-humoured brothers of Pallaskenry were to do in my own day.

And it wasn't only the brothers of Pallaskenry. Years later, in faraway Ecuador – then a brother myself – I saw Fr Peter Niceli at work in his centre for poor children. Droves of ragged children poured somewhat chaotically into that centre and Peter – who was to die prematurely of a brain tumour – taught them, fed them, clothed them and provided them with sports and entertainment (five hundred watching a film from the front of the screen, another five hundred from the back!). Above all – he loved them. Don Bosco died forty-four years before I was born, yet in Peter Niceli I saw Don Bosco.

Every threesome is perfect
In the treatment of young people, Don Bosco would stress three key factors:

1) Being reasonable: By this he means that young people should always be treated reasonably. Not often did I hear a Salesian in Pallaskenry shouting in frustration: 'You must do this because I say so!' Rather would the approach be a quietly spoken, 'Would you mind, because ...' The young are rational beings, even if parents might sometimes question this when facing one of those rampaging terrible twos!

2) Spiritual awareness: This is crucial to a young person's upbringing. We strive to pass on the faith to them; in our case this would mean helping them to come to know Jesus and the good news of salvation. In our school we didn't just hear about Jesus; we experienced him through community; we tasted the sweetness of togetherness, of being alive in Christ. Salesian spirituality can be graphically stated by saying that it is befriending one another in God. God is love (1 John 4:8), so when we befriend an-

other we are giving them an experience of God; likewise we are giving them an experience of genuine love, whose source is in God and God alone. Perhaps it was the attempts at this quality of sharing that gave my school a sense of well-being.

3) Love: While still in training as a Salesian I was assigned to South America. For a short time I stayed in a community in Dublin and there was a priest there whom I found somewhat daunting. I don't know why. I was young. As I was going up the road to catch the bus to leave for the New World, however, he ran the whole length of that long road to bid me goodbye and wish me well. Lonely as I already was, I was almost moved to tears. I had misjudged this man. That was love.

Like Don Bosco he realised that the young can only thrive in an atmosphere of loving kindness and that fear and force are destructive. As already mentioned, Bosco ruled out corporal punishment and that was 160 years ago. The English Parliament voted not to forbid smacking as a form of correction in schools as recently as 2004. Don Bosco's way was one of unfailing patience and kindness. He was deeply influenced by St Francis de Sales, who used to say, 'You can catch more flies with a spoonful of honey than with a barrel of vinegar', and 'Nothing is so strong as gentleness; nothing is so gentle as real strength.'[23] Regarding punishment, John Bosco believed that withdrawing one's smile from a child, for example, can achieve more than a smack.

Once, as a youth, I did something stupid at school. A priest whom I loved and respected said that he was disappointed in me, expected more from me. And he really did look crestfallen. I felt as though the sky had fallen in upon me.

Parents can love their children dearly yet fail to show it. This is why Don Bosco insisted that it is not enough to love young people. They must know that they are loved. They must be told that they are loved.

What John Bosco wanted in his places of education was a warm family spirit to which he also referred as the Salesian spirit.

---

23. See http://www.visitationmonastery.org/stlouis/talk_visitation_charism.htm Retrieved 25/1/04

And that is something very real. Soon after arriving in Pallaskenry as one of the new boys, I was sent to the carpenter's shop by some older lads to fetch a bottle of Salesian spirit! I obliged – and so did the carpenter! That a foundation of harmony was vital for sound education, as mentioned in the previous chapter, was something that Don Bosco knew instinctively. Does this man seem mad to you as he did to those two aloof prelates? Not to me. For his enlightened approach to education, I regard him as an inspiring educationalist: for his compassion for those who, without him, would receive no education at all, I regard him as a saint.

* * *

A Mute Inglorious Milton
In Johannesburg, I came across an extraordinary school run by a couple of Salesian sisters and some dedicated helpers. There were about 200 children in the place, ranging from nursery age to sixteen. The school taught the basics: reading, writing, and 'rithmetic. Nothing wonderful about that, you will say. But this plant was doing all it could with the resources at its disposal and, without it, these young people would receive no education at all. This allows us to see the endeavour from a totally different perspective. The students were fed at school and a cheerful atmosphere prevailed. On seeing you, the tiny tots would cry out, 'Thumb!' and you would vigorously join thumbs with them. It was their version of, 'Give me a high five!' The heart-rending shock came when you learned that 80 to 90% of these children were HIV positive. And that there were was no money for antiretroviral drugs. There were volunteer medical people who gave them homeopathic treatment, and, whereas they were listless before, this seemed to restore their energy and got them out playing football. There was the consolation that, if a now 'mute inglorious Milton' or a potential Nadine Gordimer existed among these children and survived, they would at least have the basic tools with which they could realise themselves. Don Bosco would be so proud of those Salesian sisters and their helpers.
(J.O'H)

Here is a Man
(Hymn to Don Bosco)

I
Here is a man who found a way
to make the stars above our head
seem brighter than the day.
He offered hope
he made a family of the young
by living freely, spending night and day
giving life away, finding hearts
ready to respond.

Chorus
And so we keep this memory of his life,
memory filled with joy and goodness,
reaching out to everyone, calling us to love,
bringing us to God, with a message for the world.

II
Here is a man who in his day
brought the sun to shine upon
the orphan and the stray.
His was a home,
the welcome more than you could say.
His living freely, spending night and day
giving life away, finding hearts
ready to respond.

Chorus

III
Here is a man who came to say
that love of God and brotherhood
would brighten every day.
Love was his plan, the laughter
shining in his eyes.
His living freely, spending night and day
giving life away, finding hearts
ready to respond. *Chorus (H.O'D)*

Conclusion

There are four major insights that drive the reflections in this volume. The first is that in the church we are called to be a community as the Trinity is community. This raised the intriguing questions as to what sort of a community the Trinity is and how this community model of church could be implemented. Among other features we noted, for example, that the Trinity is a community where there is:
- intimate loving and sharing,
- full participation of the three members,
- equality of persons,
- outreach in love (mission).

Regarding implementation, I noted that a practical way in which the vision of the Fathers at Vatican II is being realised is through the growth of small Christian communities that network with one another and help to make of larger scenes, such as the parish, a communion of communities.

The second insight follows on from this, declaring the primacy of the kingdom of God and its justice. This was the priority for Christ himself (cf Matthew 6:33) and as such ought to be the priority of his followers. In this context, it is important that we consider in what the kingdom of God and its justice consists. Wherever we find goodness the kingdom of God is there. Wherever there is harmony rooted in justice, the kingdom of God is to be found. And we, as Christians, give priority to upholding and supporting these. Nor does it matter who is doing the good, whether it be Jew, Christian, Muslim, Buddhist or just a concerned human being. What is the relevance of the church in this situation? It is part of the kingdom but obviously not the whole of it. However, the church should surely be at the forefront in witnessing to the kingdom, and also be a powerful instrument for building it in the world. If we would like to attract people to Christ, whom we regard as the key to our whole destiny, there is no better way than to have a church that throws its windows open to the world.

The next insight is the importance of openness. In my ministry, I have been continually challenged to open up. This is painful; we all have our constraints to overcome. In practice it has now brought me to the point where I encourage groups of all kinds, whether they be religious or civic (secular), that are doing anything to build a better world. I would have them network with, and support, one another in this endeavour. This because of the conviction that whereas reform can come from above, renewal has to come from the grassroots. This insight involves not only a vision, but also a practical strategy for achieving it.

Lastly, I went to bat on behalf of education for all; education that would set people free and not keep them 'cabin'd, cribbed, confined'. This can only be achieved against a backdrop of community. Indeed community is the ground of being for all the above aspirations, which is the reason that the imperative to love and be loved has surfaced under so many guises in this book.

The need to love and be loved has its roots deep in the Creator who *is* love. Yet, as already noted, it is often secular writers who give eloquent expression to the depths of this mystery. Raymond Carver, for example, while dying young after a difficult life – a life in which he experienced genuine love at the end – penned these lines:

And did you get what
You wanted from life even so?
I did.
And what did you want?
to call myself beloved, to feel myself
Beloved on the earth.
(*Late Fragment*)

By the same author

Small Christian Communities: Vision and Practicalities

Latest revision and update of this book of which it has been said:

'At last the book I have longed to see from the person best fitted to write it. Whatever the form of ministry, lay or ordained, I was able to recommend this major work as one filled with wisdom. For me this is the Book of the Year, a treasure and a treasure trove.'
– *Dr Ian M. Fraser, Coracle, Iona, Scotland*

'Very useful to pastors, ministers and parish councils ... much of value to say. In a work packed with theological, psychological and scriptural insights O'Halloran has succeeded in being surprisingly methodical.'
– *Brian Power, Books Ireland*

'One of the best introductions to small Christian communities.'
– *Margaret Hebblethwaite, The Tablet, England*

'Clear about the elements of a viable ecclesial community for the 21st century.'
– *Dennis Geaney, National Catholic Reporter, USA*

'Anyone seeking a vision of a renewed Church should read this book. A text of unimpeachable quality.'
– *Liam S. Maher, Hallel, Europe.*

'O'Halloran writes with the simplicity and know-how of someone who has already journeyed along the path ... Most striking is the theology of church and kingdom that undergirds the entire work ... a valuable resource for Christians who are interested in fostering educative and pastoral communities.'
– *Reviewer in Amazon.com (reviewers and customers award the book the maximum five-star rating!)*

'This book is a must.'
– *Communities Australia*

'What struck me most about the book was the author's spirituality. This is a man who is not only deeply in love with God, but also a man who experiences God's deep Trinitarian love for him.'
– *Michael O'Sullivan SJ, Milltown Studies, Ireland*

The Brendan Book of Prayer
for small groups / couples
(may be used by individuals)

'The commentaries on the Gospel passages, simply, yet profoundly written ... fresh insights into Jesus and the Gospel story. A good book for personal reflection and for the busy homilist.'

– Donal Neary SJ, The Furrow, Ireland

'An excellent follow-up to the author's book *Small Christian Communities: Vision and Practicalities* ... a lovely little volume to hold. The author's preface and poem in honour of Brendan the Navigator and the appealing cover design won this reviewer over from the outset.'

– Brian Power, Books Ireland

'Uncommon commonality...a little gem...'

– Kurt Messick, top ten reviewer, Amazon.com
(reviewers and customers award the book the maximum five-star rating!)

'A wonderful book, beautifully produced, beautifully written. There should be one in every home.'

– Gerry Glennon, Mid and North-west Radios, Ireland

'Well worth reading'

– Link Up, Dublin

'A very fine little book which all groups will find inspiring.'

– Books Editor, The Irish Catholic

'The aptly named *Brendan Book of Prayer* is beautifully produced. Any group willing to use this book will surely find nourishment and blessing on their Christian journey.'

– Brian O'Leary SJ, Milltown Studies, Ireland

BY THE SAME AUTHOR

In Search of Christ: A Prayer Book for Seekers

'... everyone who uses this book will benefit enormously, but it will provide a fine opportunity for teenagers and young adults in particular, as they think and talk about Jesus ... O'Halloran's thirty-five years' experience of fostering small groups bears eloquent fruit here ... A lovely aspect of the book is that the formula remains the same throughout, although allowing for different ingredients ... inclusive language thankfully! A good book, greatly recommended for every community.'

– Deirdre H. Whelan, Religious Life Review, Ireland

'... could be used by individuals, but could be more fruitfully used by couples, small groups of two or three, even some more.'

– Desmond Mooney, The Furrow, Ireland

'O'Halloran is clearly an experienced communicator ... He comes across as someone deeply concerned for social justice and 'the poor of the Lord'. In his piece on the Eucharist he says: "Jesus generously breaks bread with the whole world and we are challenged to do the same. This profoundly questions unbridled capitalism, for example, that engenders hunger, disease and exclusion on our planet. In short, it is not Christian ..." The perceptive Jesus Prayer makes me wish that Fr O'Halloran had used his great poetic gifts in his reflections.'

– Stephen Redmond SJ, The Irish Catholic

'This book is suitable for groups or individuals and reaches out to believers, non believers and people who want to learn more about Christ as a major historical figure.'

–Books Editor, The Universe, England

'This volume will assist those seeking, through scripture, to discover and deepen their relationship with Christ.'

– Dennis Rice, God, Christ and Us, Scotland

Amazon.com – 4.5 star-rating from reviewers and customers!

When the Acacia Bird Sings
A NOVEL

'A must for anyone who wishes to understand the pain of separation suffered by migrants and refugees. If ever a book should be on the national curriculum, this is it.'
— Tom Hyland, Irish Personality of the Year, 'Books of the Year', *The Irish Times*

'A novel of stature. I read it at a sitting, not because of its brevity – rather the story of the Machava family had gripped me intensely. Its humane perceptions remind me of Andre Brink's celebrated books. Brings the open minded reader to where literature raises timely moral questions.'
— Denis Carroll, *The Furrow*, Ireland

'This is a harrowing narrative and an epic in the classic sense, spare and stark in its prose style. There are echoes of Antigone trying to bury her dead. Very well written.'
— Rita Kelly, *Books Ireland*

'Having read *Remember José Inga!* by the same author, I was so impressed that I asked to see this book. His stories tell a truth we need to know.'
— Mary Bartholomew, *GoodBookStall* and *BBC Cumbria*, England

'The narrative is extremely well conducted and the author knows his world well. The novel will enter missionary anthologies, but why not the anthologies of literature in general?'
— *Marchés Tropicaux*, France

'O'Halloran's story has made me take a long look at my opinions and values. *When the Acacia Bird Sings* is one of those rare tales that does not force a happy ending upon us.'
— Kathy Morrissey, *Face Up, for teens*, Ireland

'A moving story of the triumph of the human spirit over appalling odds. Disturbs our smugness and forces us into guilty action to help those less fortunate.'
— Andy Pollak, *The Irish Times*

'Does for refugees what Alan Paton did for the victims of apartheid.'
— Don Mullan, author of *Eyewitness Bloody Sunday* and *The Dublin and Monaghan Bombings*, Wolfhound Press, Ireland

Amazon.com – 4.5 star-rating from reviewers and customers!

BY THE SAME AUTHOR

Remember José Inga!
A NOVEL

'A good novel. Yes! But so much more.'
— *Mary Bartholomew, GoodBookStall and BBC Cumbria, England*

'Having read *Remember José Inga!* by the same author, I was so impressed that I asked to see *When the Acacia Bird Sings*.'
— *Mary Bartholomew, GoodBookStall and BBC Cumbria, England*

'This novel describes graphically the sometimes brutal forces that keep people in poverty and the gigantic struggle it is for those who are oppressed to change their situation ... The general reader will find *Remember José Inga!* deeply engaging and it will be of particular interest to people committed to peace and justice, who will find this book hugely informative and inspiring.'
— *Shay Claffey, St Anthony's Messenger, Ireland*

Amazon.com – 4.5 star-rating from reviewers and customers!

The Least of These
A book of short stories

'O'Halloran writes with a shrewd eye and accurate ear, catching and holding the reader's attention with some startlingly precise images and with dialogue so natural and accurate the reader feels at times as if he were eavesdropping on the characters of these tales ... a skilled collection by a gifted writer.'

– *Brendan Kennelly, Trinity College, Dublin*

'Highlights a variety of issues at the core of justice and peace in an easy, attractive way that immediately engages the sympathy of the reader ... the language is simple and beautiful, the stories very moving ... The volume is warm and human, based on a life at the front line.'

– *Alo Donnelly, Executive Director, Concern Universal*

All the foregoing books are available at:

Email: info@columba.ie (Ireland)
Email: mail@durnell.co.uk (Europe)
Email: info@dufoureditions.com (USA)
Email: cservice@novalis.ca (Canada)
Email: rba@rainbowbooks.co.au (Australia)
Email: catholic.supplies@clear.net.nz (New Zealand)